Douglas Bowie
Two Plays

Goodbye, Piccadilly
Rope's End

Douglas Bowie
Two Plays

Goodbye, Piccadilly

Rope's End

Playwrights Canada Press

Toronto • Canada

Playwrights Canada Press
The Canadian Drama Publisher
215 Spadina Avenue, Suite 230, Toronto, Ontario CANADA M5T 2C7
416-703-0013 fax 416-408-3402
orders@playwrightscanada.com • www.playwrightscanada.com

This book would be twice its cover price were it not for the support of Canadian taxpayers through the Government of Canada Book Publishing Industry Development Programme, the Canada Council for the Arts, the Ontario Arts Council, and the Ontario Media Development Corporation.

Front cover image by Bianca de Blok
Cover design by Blake Sproule
Production Editor: JLArt & Micheline Courtemanche

Library and Archives Canada Cataloguing in Publication

Bowie, Douglas
Douglas Bowie : two plays : Goodbye, Piccadilly and Rope's end / Douglas Bowie.

ISBN 978-0-88754-791-1

I. Bowie, Douglas. Goodbye, Piccadilly. II. Bowie, Douglas. Rope's end. III. Title.

PS8603.O9757D69 2008 C812'.6 C2008-902300-5

First edition: October 2008
Printed and bound by Canadian Printco at Scarborough, Canada.

Song Credits

For the three women in my life

Joan

Alison

And in memory of my mother

Catharine (1915 – 2007)

Contents

Goodbye, Piccadilly

Introduction

What kick-starts the creative process? People sometimes say to me that they have tons of good ideas but just can't "write them down." Well, sure, writing them down is hard, but I find good ideas are a scarce commodity as well. When I'm asked where mine come from, usually all I can honestly say is that I don't have a clue. But, as Bess says in *Goodbye, Piccadilly*, people expect a "proper answer," and so…

Chatting with my friend Peter Peart, he tells me he nominated a man – a World War II vet – for the Order of Canada, and the fellow is going to get it. I hadn't realized that you, or I, or anyone can nominate someone, and they may actually get the thing – our highest honour. Interesting, but I think no more of it, and spend the ensuing weeks scribbling on an idea for a TV thing. There's a possibility of a Canadian-British co-production, and I have a vague notion for a series called "The Retreat". It would revolve around a "great man" – a once famous actor who comes from England to a run-down lodge in Canada. From there he plans to dispense high culture to unwashed colonials for a price. There's a dark secret in his past that he's escaping from but, of course, the Canadians won't know that.

But somehow the idea doesn't catch fire. How much fresh mileage is there, really, in a culture clash between hoity-toity Brits and dumb-ass Canadians? I find my mind drifting back to Peter's story, musing about the World War II vet who's getting the Order of Canada. Wondering about the other names that appear on the list each year. Who are they? Unknown to us, but pillars of their communities, surely. What are their stories?

I scribble a fateful sentence – "What if someone from town, the mayor, is the owner of the lodge" – and my whole idea gets turned on its head. Suddenly my "great man" is not British, but quintessentially Canadian, a war hero, Mr. Volunteer, a small-town mayor whose life culminates with a phone call announcing that he's been awarded the Order of Canada. But who is he, really? What are his secrets?

The scribbled notes come faster now. The run down lodge becomes a country inn, owned by this man and his wife for half a century. Fragmentary ideas pile up – "canoe trip, Algonquin Park" – "bomber pilot, wounded" – "fiftieth anniversary of VE Day," "Vera Lynn" – "(There'll be Bluebirds Over) The White Cliffs of Dover" – and more.

And names. I can't write a character until I know in my bones who he is, until I know his name. A lot of World War II pilots had nicknames – Cap, Punch, Red. I almost settle on Babe but it never looks quite right on the page, and there's that pig movie. So who is this guy anyway? He's a pillar of a community, he's a rock, he's a – Brick.

His wife, whom I've tentatively named Marge, I change to Bess. They have a daughter, a bit of a tomboy, so a boyish name, Samantha, Ricky – Roberta. And the Brickley family is born – Brick, Bess and Bobbie. And a theme starts to emerge as well, because in the end this becomes a story about family – how we lose them, where we find them, the deep-rooted need to be part of one.

After my handwritten notes reach seventy pages, I finally turn on the computer and start to write. Sometimes I write out of order, tackling a scene here, a scene there. But that's often a sign of trouble, that I don't really know what my story's about. One of the best writing tips I've come across is to "feel the ground moving beneath your feet" – to feel the story going forward as you write. But that's not easy. Every writer gets stuck, and there's no justice. The sticking points, the scenes you sweat and labour over for weeks are apt to feel sweaty and laboured when they're done. The ones dashed off with (relative) ease often retain a sense of that ease in the end.

So, still thinking in terms of a TV thing, I start at the beginning, describe Bess rushing in and grabbing the phone, and launch into her opening speech – "Yes!… Oh, Marge, sorry. I didn't mean to bark, but it's been a madhouse here!…" I can hear her voice in my head. The speech flows (and will end up on stage a year later with only minor changes). But when it reaches two and a half pages it strikes me – a two and a half page speech? In a TV script where three lines is the norm? Maybe what I'm writing here is a play. Didn't I vow I'd never do that again?

But indeed, many months later, a play is what it turns out to be – a play called *Goodbye, Piccadilly.* My daughter, Alison, asks why I didn't call it "Farewell, Leicester Square" which actually ties in more closely with events in the story, but I just didn't, that's all.

Douglas Bowie
September 2007

Goodbye, Piccadilly was first performed at the Thousand Islands Playhouse, Gananoque, on May 9, 2002 with the following company:

Cecil Beauregard "Brick" Brickley	Mo Bock
Bess Brickley	Heather Esdon
Roberta "Bobbie" Brickley	Tracey Ferencz
A Man	Matthew Gibson
Kitty McCooey	Meg Walter

Directed by Greg Wanless
Set Designed by Carolyn M. Smith
Costumes by Anne Redish
Lighting by Tim Fort
Stage Managed by Kirsti Bruce

• • •

Goodbye, Piccadilly opened at the Blyth Festival on July 3, 2002 with the following company:

Cecil Beauregard "Brick" Brickley	Bob Nasmith
Bess Brickley	Janet Amos
Roberta "Bobbie" Brickley	Caroline Gillis
A Man	John Jarvis
Kitty McCooey	Elva Mai Hoover

Directed by Diana Belshaw
Sets and Costumes by Shawn Kerwin
Lighting by Renee Brodie
Stage Managed by Jennifer Jansen

• • •

NOTE: *Goodbye, Piccadilly* was originally discussed as a co-production between the Thousand Islands Playhouse and the Blyth Festival. In the end this proved to be impractical, and two separate productions were staged.

Characters

CECIL BEAUREGARD "BRICK" BRICKLEY, age 75
BESS BRICKLEY, Brick's wife, age 73
ROBERTA "BOBBIE" BRICKLEY, their daughter, age 47
KITTY McCOOEY, age 71
A MAN, fiftyish

Setting

The play takes place in and around The Spinney, a small country inn in a town in Canada. The story begins in November, 2000, and continues over the ensuing year and more.

Acknowledgements

Unlike a novel or epic poem, a play requires actors' voices to nourish it and help it to flower. I'd like to thank the generous performers who participated in workshops, offered suggestions and contributed to the development of *Goodbye, Piccadilly*: Matthew Gibson, Mo Bock, David Fox, Brooke Johnson, Jill Hodkinson, Laurel Paetz, Heather Bonham, John Jarvis and Robin Craig.

Special thanks to Damir Andrei for his friendly help and suggestions on the script, Heather Esdon who proposed a useful structural change during rehearsals (a change I stubbornly resisted but finally incorporated to the benefit of the play), Sue Perkins for her enthusiastic advocacy of the play and Janet Amos, a consummate pro, who rescued us in a pinch.

Goodbye, Piccadilly would not have come to pass without the enthusiastic support of Anne Chislett, Artistic Director of the Blyth Festival and Greg Wanless, Artistic Director of the Thousand Islands Playhouse. My huge thanks to them as well.

Pre Show

A woman (KITTY) sings a medley of some of the more evocative WWII songs – "(There'll be Bluebirds Over) The White Cliffs of Dover", "We'll Meet Again" and "Lilli Marlene".

A man (BRICK) accompanies her on the piano, not a pro, but someone who can play a tune or two.

(Note: The pre-show is optional. Alternatively we could hear recordings of World War II songs – Vera Lynn, Glenn Miller or the like.)

At curtain time – the lighting changes, isolating KITTY in a pool of "memory light." She sings, perhaps "I'll Be Seeing You In All the Old Familiar Places".

She's interrupted by the sound of Churchill's distinctive voice on a crackly radio, announcing that the German High Command has surrendered. The war in Europe is over.

KITTY reacts with elation, laughing, hugging (unseen) people.

BRICK's reaction is quite different. He sits there, almost stunned – then gets up and slips away. After a moment, KITTY notices he's missing, looks around curiously.

We begin to hear the shrill ringing of a phone as light the shifts.

Act One

Scene One

The basic set is the main sitting room and reception area of The Spinney – a small country inn with a comfortable wood-panelled, country-craftsy feeling about it, such as one might find in any number of Canadian towns.

There's a reception desk, a main entrance door, a hallway and staircase (or two?) to other parts of the inn – but this may be more of a suggestive set with certain key props, such as the piano and some conventional landscape and wildlife prints on the walls, rather than a fully-dressed, naturalistic one.

We also need a sense of a couple of downstage playing areas which are not part of the main set, where scenes away from the inn will occur. The location of these scenes – a church, a lawyer's office, etc. are indicated in the scene headings as an aid to the reader. Again, these settings will be merely suggestive – chairs, a table, the odd telling prop.

The phone continues to ring.

BESS *(off)* I'm coming!

BESS rushes in. She's seventy if she's a day, but still quick-witted, sharp as a tack and at the moment, a bundle of harried energy. She grabs the phone impatiently.

The Spinney B&B!… Oh, Marge, sorry. I didn't mean to bark, but it's been a madhouse here! You'll never guess who I just got off the line with. Dave Stevens!… Of course you know who Dave Stevens is! CBC. Radio Noon. Ed Lawrence. The gardening phone-in…. No, no. I didn't call about my gloxinias. He called here! Looking for Brick! – He's been awarded the Order of Canada!… Not Dave! *Brick!*… Yes! The blessed phone has been ringing non-stop!… Oh, he doesn't know yet. He left yesterday on his damn-fool canoe trip into the wilds of Algonquin Park…. I know. A seventy-five-year-old man. Alone in a canoe in November. It's foolishness, but we've done it this way forever. I go off on my yoga retreat. He goes off into the forest primeval to get in touch with his inner paddle. We spend every day together fifty-one weeks a year. One week apart is probably good for us, and the truth is I don't even start missing him until the fourth or fifth hour. I know. It's so sappy. I don't know how people can stand us…. Going to the ceremony?! Of course I'm going! How often will I get to hobnob with Governor General Adrienne Clarkson – and John – I really should try and read one of those books of his. Voltaire's Buggers or whatever it's called. I've got it around here somewhere. They've already sent us an email from Ottawa with all sorts of instructions about how to address Adrienne – a deep curtsy and a heartfelt "your Majesty" will do nicely *(almost giggly)*…. Brick? Oh, he'll pooh-pooh it, but he'll be pleased, deep down. He'll have one of his fits, though, because the citation calls him *Cecil*! No one's called him Cecil since Miss Whittle in grade six!

The line beeps.

Oops, there's the other line again. Probably Adrienne wondering what I'm going to wear. Hang on—

Presses the button.

Order of Canada Central.... Yes, this is the residence of Cecil Beauregard Brickley.... You're calling from where?... *Really?* Hold on a sec—

Presses the button.

It's London, Marge – *England!* I better take it. *(laughing)* It may be the Palace! Look, come to Toronto with me and help me pick out a dress. We'll take the club car and drink Drambuie. My treat. Next week. I'll call you.

Presses the button.

Sorry to keep you waiting. This is Mrs. Cecil Brickley. I expect you're looking for my husband. He's known as Brick by the way.... *(listening, slightly puzzled)* No, no. You don't understand. My husband's not in England. He's in Algonquin Park. Here in the colonies. Paddling. *(silence)* No, no, no. You're not making sense. That's quite impossible... *(longer silence)* Well, it's obviously a different Cecil Beauregard Brickley. It's not an uncommon name.... His wallet? But?... *Please stop saying you're sorry!* I have no idea who that is, but it cannot possibly be my husband! He drove away yesterday with a canoe on top of his car! You think – you think a man who's going to England would spend an hour putting a canoe on his car? The very idea is ludicrous. You don't *canoe* in England. You punt – or whatever. This is all some horrible – dreadful—

The line beeps again.

—mistake—

Presses the button, dazed.

Yes.... Who is this?... Oh, hello, Bobbie, dear. I'm sorry. Of course I recognize your voice. I'm just distracted.... Your father – your father – your father has won the Order of Canada.

Brownout.

BESS remains sitting in the half light. She looks numb, and very much her age. The phone keeps ringing, janglingly. She doesn't move, doesn't seem to hear it – lost.

BOBBIE comes in, puts down her bags. She's mid-fortyish, trim, athletic, tomboyish. Almost a sense of slow motion here, two characters under water emotionally. Mother and daughter embrace wordlessly, stand holding each other.

BRICK materializes out of shadows. He's seventy-five, as we've heard, but solid and fit-looking, salt of the earth. He comes forward and hugs them both. They don't know he's there.

Blackout.

Scene Two – The Inn (A couple of days later)

The room is awash in fresh flowers now – in several vases, and piled on tables and chairs.

BESS is standing on a chair, looking in an upper cabinet as BOBBIE comes downstairs.

BOBBIE Mum?

BESS *(distressed, fussing)* I know we have other vases somewhere, that purple one.

BOBBIE Please get down—

BESS But people will be coming by. They'll expect to see their flowers.

BOBBIE helps her down, at once impatient and gentle. BESS seems older somehow, overwhelmed.

The kitchen is full of them. We can't just let them die.

BOBBIE I'll take care of the flowers later, Mum. We have to go.

BESS You know the vase I mean. It's more puce than purple. It's really quite ugly—

BOBBIE *(trying to get her moving towards the door)* Mum, please. The visitation starts in five minutes.

BESS *(stops)* Yes. Now if anyone asks, Brick still gets the Order of Canada. I had a lovely letter from the Governor General, who said she hoped I'd still come to the ceremony, so I'll still have to buy a dress. *(stops again)* Maybe I should get it—

BOBBIE What?

BESS The letter. People may want to see it.

BOBBIE For God's sake, Mother! No one will care about the Order of Canada! They'll want to know what he was doing in England! On a bench in Leicester Square, like some homeless—

BESS *Stop it!* I don't know! – I don't know – *(breaking down)* I don't know—

BOBBIE I'm sorry – I'm sorry— *(sighs, hugs her)*

BESS I used to worry so; every November. It was always the same. He'd preside at the Remembrance Day service, lay a wreath for his old squadron, and the next day he'd take off by himself with that damn canoe. What if he had another heart attack? What if it tipped? He'd freeze to death. He'd call out, but there'd be no one to hear, no one to help him.... Do you think he called out? Do you think people just walked by – left him lying there?

BOBBIE I don't know, Mum. It doesn't bear thinking about.

BESS Why didn't he take me? I would have loved to go to London. I've never been there. Never been anywhere. And if I'd been with him, maybe I could have...

BOBBIE tries to get her moving, but BESS stops again, faltering, as if she can't face it.

Maybe he had some sort of Alzheimer's episode. He'd been awfully absent-minded lately. He went to the ATM last week and deposited a prescription for Tylenol Number Three. Maybe he got confused and—

BOBBIE It's pretty hard to confuse Algonquin Park with Leicester Square.

BESS But everyone will be wondering, whispering in the corners. What was he doing there? We have to say *something!*

BOBBIE We'll tell the truth. We don't have the faintest idea.

BESS The truth? Don't be silly. People will expect a proper answer. *(trying to think)* We'll say – we'll say he went over for the fiftieth anniversary of the end of the war—

BOBBIE That was five years ago!

BESS Well, all right – the fifty-fifth anniversary.

BOBBIE Dammit, Mum! He's dead and we're cooking up a *cover story!* Don't you want to know what happened?!

BESS *(silence)* I don't know. Do I?

BRICK appears in the background now, and it's almost as if this is addressed to him.

He remains there, listening, reacting with a sense of both guilt and frustration – as if he'd like to intervene, to make this right – but, of course, he can't.

BOBBIE Well, I'm not going to look people in the eye – people who've known me since I was a little girl – and lie to them.

BESS Don't call it lying. It's – it's doing what's necessary.

BOBBIE Keeping up appearances? At all costs?

BESS Yes! Your father and I are – are public figures in this town. We've lived our whole lives here. I refuse to stand there in front of everyone and admit – I don't even know what I'm admitting.... Won't you just do it? For me? You'd do it for him. In a flash.

BOBBIE But Dad would never ask me to lie. Lying was the one thing he wouldn't stand for, as a matter of principle.

BESS You're a fine one to talk about principles! What drawer did you stick them in when you took your marriage vows? Divorced three times! It's disgraceful. And your father thought so, too.

BOBBIE Divorced twice. The third one hasn't gone through yet. I'm still married to Bruce. Technically.

BESS And what's so wrong with him?

BOBBIE *(shrugs)* He's no Brick Brickley.

BESS Well, most people by your age – most *adults* – learn you sometimes have to settle for half a loaf in this life.

BOBBIE Right. That's how Bruce stole my heart. When he promised to love, honour, and be half a loaf.

BRICK chuckles, then reacts, almost surprised that he can make a sound.

BESS And where has that sort of attitude got you? Forty-seven years old. Alone in the world. No husband. No children. No one who cares about you—

BOBBIE *(quietly)* I thought you cared about me, Mum.

BESS *(silence)* I do. And if you care about me, you'll do as I ask.

BOBBIE But it's a matter of—

BESS Don't say it's a matter of principle! There are things in this world that are more important than principles!

BOBBIE Like what?

BESS Like doing what your mother says!

BOBBIE I just don't think I can.

BESS Fine. Don't come.

BOBBIE Fine. I won't.

BESS goes to the door.

BRICK *(suddenly blurts)* No, Bess. Wait.

BRICK reacts, again surprised that he can speak. BESS pauses by the door – and for a second BRICK may think he's caused this, turns to BOBBIE.

This is my fault. Don't take it out on her—

But BESS has only paused to take her coat. She goes out.

(to BOBBIE) Do as your mother asks.

But BOBBIE turns away and heads for the stairs.

Do as your father asks.

BOBBIE pauses for just a beat – is she sensing his presence, or just feeling guilty? – then continues up the stairs.

Bobbie… Roberta Brickley!

But she's gone. BRICK stands there, visibly frustrated.

Light shifts.

Scene Three – Funeral Parlour

BESS reappears, stands alone in a pool of light – shaking hands, exchanging hugs, murmurs, with unseen people, as if in a receiving line.

BESS Thank you – Yes, he was, thanks so much…. Algonquin Park? Yes, well, he decided to skip that this year because he – he always wanted to go back to London. You see, he talked about it – constantly – endlessly – all the time—

She looks vulnerable, shaky. BRICK crosses and stands watching, trying to provide moral support, pained that he can't help.

—and what with the fifty – the fifty-fifth anniversary of the end of the war, the celebrations—

BRICK Is *that* the best she can do? Good Lord.

BESS Oh, it was a big thing – the fifty-fifth, Vera Lynn and – and all that.... What exactly happened? Well, I – that is he, uh – *(foundering)* it's difficult to explain – exactly – it's—

BRICK *(impotent)* It's none of their damn business.

BESS *(on the verge of breaking down)* —it's, it's—

BOBBIE *(entering)* It's something we'd rather not discuss just now. *(She squeezes her mother's arm reassuringly.)* You understand.

She takes her place beside her mother, and we sense BESS steadying, taking strength from her daughter's presence. We see BRICK's reaction – pleased, and just a shade curious whether he had anything to do with this or not.

BESS You understand.

BOBBIE It's just too—

BESS It's just too—

BOBBIE —you know.

BESS You know.

BOBBIE Why did he go?

BESS Why didn't I go?

BOBBIE Well, he – he—

BESS Well, I – I—

BOBBIE He – wanted to see his old pals.

BESS I'd just have been in the way—

BOBBIE —hoist a few single malts—

BESS —a wet blanket—

BOBBIE —tell a few lies. *(realizes what she's said)* I don't mean lies literally. Dad certainly wasn't a liar – I mean, you know, tall stories, war stories—

BRICK Lies.

BESS He wanted to visit his old stomping grounds—

Light up on KITTY (still in mid-forties fashion) in the background, humming softly – "Tipperary". BRICK turns and looks – the only one who sees her, as if this is taking place in his mind.

BOBBIE Piccadilly Circus—

KITTY *(singing softly, emotionally)* "It's a long way to Tipperary—"

BESS Trafalgar Square—

KITTY "It's a long way to go—"

BOBBIE The Old Bull and Bush—

KITTY "It's a long way to Tipperary
To the sweetest girl I know—"

BESS Leicester Square—*(almost breaking down, hugging an unseen person, whispering)* Oh, Marge. I have no idea – no idea what he was doing there.

KITTY "Goodbye, Piccadilly,
Farewell, Leicester Square—"

BOBBIE takes her mother's arm, supports her, helps her off.

BRICK stands there, looking from KITTY to BESS, as if he doesn't know which way to turn.

(smiles at BRICK) Cheer up, luv. The war's over.

Lights slowly fade on BESS and BOBBIE as they go, mouthing words silently to unseen people.

"It's a long, long way to Tipperary,
But my heart's right there."

BRICK remains standing there as the light slowly fades and shifts.

Scene Four – The Inn

BESS and BOBBIE come back in, looking exhausted. BOBBIE supports her, holding her arm.

BOBBIE Did Dad know everyone in the county?

BESS And their brothers. Thank you for doing that, dear—*(gives her daughter an emotional hug)* You're all I have left of him now.

BOBBIE returns the hug, leads her to the stairs.

(stops) The flowers—

BOBBIE Oh, screw the – I mean, I'll take care of the flowers. You're going to bed. *(guides her mother up the stairs)* We've got another long day tomorrow.

BESS *(as they go)* That purple vase must be around somewhere.

During this, there's a discreet knock at the door, then another.

BOBBIE *(off)* I'll find it. You get some sleep.

BESS *(off)* Your father never liked it. He called it the Purple Vase of Cairo.

BOBBIE comes back downstairs. She looks almost as drained as her mother, musing aloud.

BOBBIE So you knew everyone in the county, Dad; but did they know you? Did they know you?

She picks up a bunch of flowers.

A man's face peers in a window. BOBBIE sees it, screams.

BESS *(off, calls down)* Roberta?! Are you all right?

The man signals frantically, apologetically, trying to indicate that he's harmless.

BOBBIE *(calls)* I'm fine! Go to sleep!

She opens the door. A man in his early fifties is standing there, holding a liquor bag. He's well-dressed in a tailored suit, a carnation in the buttonhole. He has a subtle British accent and an ever so slightly fey manner.

MAN I'm dreadfully sorry. I did knock. Several times.

BESS *(off)* Is someone there? Is it Bruce?!

BOBBIE No, it's not Bruce! It's – uh—?

MAN McCooey—

BOBBIE It's Mr. McCooey!

BESS *(off)* Orm's boy?

He shakes his head.

BOBBIE No! A different McCooey!

MAN *(hands her the liquor bag a bit awkwardly)* I know a casserole is rather *de rigeur* on these occasions – and actually I do a *cassoulet de canard* that your dad was very fond of—

BESS *(off)* We don't know any other McCooeys!

BOBBIE *Go to sleep*, mother!

MAN —but it doesn't travel well, and I thought under the circumstances this might be more – utilitarian.

BOBBIE *(checks the bottle)* Lagavulin? You're a man after my dad's own heart. He liked his single malt.

MAN He did indeed.

BOBBIE Well, thank you.

MAN You're welcome, Bobbie.

BOBBIE I'm sorry. Should I know you?

MAN No, no. You shouldn't. Well—*(hesitates, uncomfortable)* Look, I know it's late, and you've had a hellish couple of days, but I'd rather like to talk to you – if—

BOBBIE Sorry, I'm out on my feet. This death business is exhausting.

MAN It is that. I'm knackered myself. Jet lag. Beastly flight over. Crammed in beside some tedious marmalade salesman from Chipping Norton—

BOBBIE Chipping Norton? That's in—

MAN *Almost* in the Cotswolds. It's Cotswoldish, but it doesn't have that creamy, postcardy feel to it. Mind you—

BOBBIE *(cuts him off)* Did I hear you correctly before? Did you say that Dad was fond of your—?

MAN My *cassoulet.* Loved it. He called it duck stew, but that was just to twit me.

BOBBIE And, and where would he have had that – exactly?

MAN In London. *Chez moi.*

BOBBIE *(glances around to make sure there's no sign of her mother)* Well, suddenly I seem to be awake. I guess you'd better come in.

MAN *(comes in, looks around)* Just like he described it. Except for the – art?

BOBBIE *(cuts him off again)* So, London. So – do you know what happened? When he—

MAN Oh, yes. I was there – when he – that is, almost there. Actually, I was just around the corner getting us lattes. It sounds so bloody banal, doesn't it? Was it Henry James who said—?

BOBBIE I don't have the faintest idea.

MAN Sorry. I'm a blatherer. And you don't appreciate being the blatheree. You want to hear about it.

BOBBIE *(eyeing him slightly askance)* Do I?

MAN Oh, it really wasn't that bad – I mean, it was a nightmare, of course. He was much too young to die. Still so bloody robust. When I met him at Heathrow, he threw his arms around me, squeezed me half to death.

She stares at him – promptly cracks open the Lagavulin, goes and pours herself a stiff belt, knocks it back, gasps.

BOBBIE Continue.

MAN Where was I?

BOBBIE Being squeezed half to death.

MAN Sorry – an unhappy choice of words. Anyway, I thought he looked a little peaked. That overnight flight is barbaric, and he wasn't a relaxed flier, so I said come on home and put your head down for a couple of hours, but he only had the week. So nothing would do but we had to beetle down to Leicester Square and get half-price tickets for a matinee. We enjoy a good musical, anything but the dreaded Andrew Lloyd, although *Joseph* is charming in a derivative sort of—

She just fixes him with a look of intense impatience.

Sorry. I'm a bit nervous. So, I left him in the queue, and when I came back with the lattes, he'd vanished. And my first reaction was, where have you got to, you old silly? Your latte will get cold… and then I saw him. Lying on a bench. Do you know Leicester Square? It's a bit tacky, but not awful. The sun was shining, a busker was playing "Send in the Clowns", and he was just lying there, peacefully, the tickets in his hand. I thought he'd fallen asleep… but, well – he wasn't asleep. I started hollering for help, pounding on his chest, trying to give him CPR, but I'm just hopeless at practical things like that. He always twitted me about it – said I couldn't change a tire to save my life. Turned out I couldn't do CPR to save his – I've never felt so bloody helpless, blubbering like a baby, screaming at him to wake up, please wake up. But he didn't.

He trails off, almost in tears. BOBBIE is moved too, uncomfortable.

BOBBIE So – well, thank you—

MAN For nothing.

BOBBIE For trying.

MAN He couldn't have suffered. It was so quick. One minute he was laughing, chatting away, excited to be there – and the next…

BOBBIE Well, it's good to know – he didn't suffer – but—

MAN But what a shock. I know. He was still so full of life. When he gave me that hug at the airport I thought I'd faint.

BOBBIE Yes. You mentioned that already. Well, thank you again, Mr. McCooey. Really. This has been most – most, uh – informative—

She tries to ease him toward the door.

MAN There is more. Information.

BOBBIE Somehow I sensed that. Oh, I know. We're all sophisticated adults here. We know a fine single malt from a pedestrian blend. So. Are you saying? – Are you telling me? – Come on, Bobbie – Are you telling me that you're his – that you and he are – were – uh—

She gulps her Scotch, can't bring herself to say it…. Silence…. More silence…

You know—

MAN You know?

BOBBIE You know.

MAN *(realizing what she means)* You – No, no, no, no, no, no, no, no. *No!* Oh, God. What in the world gave you an idea like that?!

BOBBIE I can't imagine.

MAN No, no–

BOBBIE Oh, thank God.

She pours herself another Scotch and gulps it down.

MAN I'm his *son!*

She gags, spewing Scotch.

Sorry. I thought it would be a shock – I wanted to ease into it.

BOBBIE Oooh, you eased into it all right. In all my born days, I've seldom seen a better job of easing into.

MAN *(offers his hand)* Cecil McCooey.

She takes his hand as the new reality begins to sink in. His son?

BOBBIE Wait a minute. Cecil? You mean Ceecil?

CECIL We say Cecil. As in Rhodes. As in B. deMille. Ceecil sounds a bit like fingernails on slate.

BOBBIE Are you a foundling?

CECIL I beg your—?

BOBBIE *(the Scotch starting to go to her head)* Were you left on his doorstep? I mean, you don't *look* like him. You don't *sound* like him. At all.... Maybe you're some sort of con artist! I've heard about people like you, reading the obits, preying on widows and orphans when they're addled with grief—

He's at a loss for words. Is she serious?

Ceecil indeed! You've been just a hair too clever with the name thing, Ceecil boy! You see, my father detested that name with a holy passion—

CECIL Oh, I—

BOBBIE And if he'd ever had a little bastard son – which he didn't – he would've named him – Priscilla before he named him Ceecil. Which in your case might have been a better fit.

CECIL *(unfazed)* But he didn't name me. My mum did. He didn't even know about me 'til I was six. Imagine finding out you not only have a son, but a son named Cecil. Poor chap. So he always called me Sonny.

BOBBIE Not Cher?

CECIL *(not bothered at all, laughs)* You're just so – right. He adored you, but you know that. Even after all the divorces—

BOBBIE *(drinking)* Oh, shut up.

CECIL We have a picture of you on the mantle at home, you know.

BOBBIE *(rolls her eyes)* And what do you say when people ask who it is?

CECIL *(quietly)* I say she's my sister.

Silence. She has no smart retort to this. He takes an envelope from his pocket.

I anticipated your skepticism, so I brought some snaps.

BOBBIE Oh, goody.

CECIL *(hands her some photos)* Dad and I at the London Zoo, at Madame Tussaud's. Tacky. Give it a miss. Outside the Palace Theatre after we saw *Les Miz.* Have you seen it?

BOBBIE glances at the pictures half-heartedly and shakes her head.

Oh you have to! We'll go some time.

She looks at him as if he's crazy.

Sorry, I'm overstepping. I'm just excited to finally meet you, that's all—

BOBBIE Likewise, I'm sure.

CECIL Oh, I understand. To you, I'm nothing. I didn't exist until, well, now. But to me, you're the sister I've known about, wondered about for all these years, and you're just the way I thought you'd be. You're just… perfect.

BOBBIE Should see me when I haven't just spent four hours at a funeral home—

CECIL And ten minutes in the Lagavulin.

BOBBIE *(almost laughs)* Look, Ceecil—

CECIL Cecil, but call me Sonny.

BOBBIE Dream on. Look, let's say, for the sake of argument, that I believe you, *(gives him back the photos)* but what possible purpose is served by this? Other than destroying his memory for us, sullying his name—

CECIL That's the last thing—

BOBBIE Why couldn't you just have stayed home? Left us in blissful ignorance?

CECIL He was my father. We loved him. We weren't going to send him back alone. In a box.

BOBBIE We?

CECIL Kitty and I.

BOBBIE Kitty?

CECIL My mum. She's here too.

BOBBIE *(shoots a horrified glance at the window)* Here?!

CECIL Not *here,* here. Down the road. At a rather unsatisfactory motel.

BOBBIE Why?

CECIL Well, I knew you were closed. That's why he always came in November.

BOBBIE Always?

CECIL Every year for forty-eight years.

BOBBIE *(half to herself)* No wonder that canoe was in such good shape.

CECIL Never missed a year – except in '84. When he had the bypass surgery—

BOBBIE *Oh stop it!* Dropping these little personal details! He wasn't a relaxed flier! We liked musicals! Bypass surgery! As if you sat up through the night at the hospital wondering if he'd live or die! As if he was really your father! As if it was anything more than a – a technical thing! The result of some meaningless little wartime – spasm!

CECIL *(He looks as if he's been slapped. Silence)* He was a good father to me. A loving father – coming to see us without fail for forty-eight years, supporting us, calling on birthdays. I don't call that spasmodic. I call it fatherly.

BOBBIE *(slightly apologetically)* Look. Thanks for this. *(lifts the Lagavulin)* Thanks for everything. End of story. This will be our little secret. There's no earthly reason why my mother has to know any of this.

CECIL I tend to agree, but there's another—

BOBBIE No! No buts! If you have an ounce of British decency, an ounce of sensitivity – which you obviously do – you'll go out that door and vanish into the night.

She drains her drink, ushers him towards the door.

CECIL But I'm afraid it's not quite that—

BOBBIE *(losing patience)* Look, my mother is an old woman – well, oldish – and I'll be damned if she's going to hear one goddam word about this! Good night!

She practically pushes him out and closes the door.

Shit!

She turns and is startled to see her mother standing at the foot of the stairs, where she's evidently been listening. She's holding a strikingly ugly purple vase.

BESS I found it.

She suddenly looks faint. BOBBIE dashes to her, catches her – and the vase – just as she collapses in a swoon.

Lights shift.

Scene Five — A Church

We hear soft organ music, perhaps "Abide With Me".

BRICK comes on downstage beside his own coffin (on wheels), as if he's a pallbearer at his own funeral. A grumpy, troubled one at that.

BRICK *(feeling the wood)* Waste of money. I told you I wanted to be cremated. *(looks around, surveying the turnout)* Don't you people have anything better to do?

BESS and BOBBIE come in, arm in arm, take seats downstage, as if in the first row.

BRICK tenses as he sees KITTY and CECIL enter at the back. (KITTY, now in contemporary dress, is two or three years younger than BESS, and a bit softer somehow, less substantial, more ethereal.) They look around for seats and come toward the front.

BESS *(incredulous, in a church whisper)* Is that—?

BOBBIE I guess so.

BRICK *(to CECIL and KITTY)* Maybe it would be better if you sat—

They take seats right across the aisle from BESS and BOBBIE, CECIL closest to BOBBIE.

—at the back.

BESS can't help glancing at them, venom mixed with curiosity. KITTY glances at them as well – curiosity without the venom.

KITTY Is that—?

CECIL nods.

BESS Do they have to sit in the front row?!

BOBBIE They're the only empty seats, Mum. The place is jammed. Just ignore them. No one knows who they are.

CECIL *(leans across to BOBBIE, church whisper) Quel* turnout. It's a wonderful tribute to him.

BRICK Agh, they're just here for the free lunch.

BOBBIE ignores CECIL, but he leans over, gesturing that he has more to say.

CECIL *(whispers)* Bobbie—

She keeps her eyes straight ahead. Undeterred, CECIL eases over, hunkers in the aisle beside her. BOBBIE is stuck there, unable to avoid him. (The following is conducted in variations of church whispers and hisses.)

Sorry. Really. I feel like the relative from hell.

BOBBIE *(alarmed that someone will hear)* Shhh! Don't use that word!

CECIL Hell?

BOBBIE *(hissing)* Relative!

BESS sits uncomfortably, trying at once to ignore him, and yet to hear what he says.

CECIL But I felt I should forewarn you. Before tomorrow—

BOBBIE Tomorrow? What's tomorrow?

CECIL Well, the, uh, reading—

BRICK Not now, Sonny—

CECIL —of the will.

BRICK flinches. Silence. BOBBIE just looks at CECIL, incredulous.

BESS What?

BOBBIE Shhh!

CECIL We understand – that is, he told us – Dad—

BOBBIE *Shhh!*

BRICK *(to CECIL)* Not here—

BESS What?

CECIL —that he made some small provision – for Kitty and me.

BOBBIE He *didn't!*

BESS Shhhh! Didn't what?

CECIL —in the will.

BOBBIE *Why?!*

CECIL Shhhh!

BESS Why what?

CECIL It's something he just felt the need to do, I suppose.

BOBBIE Let's not talk about what he felt the *need* to do, all right?!

BESS Shhhh!

BOBBIE Let's just not go there!

BESS Where!?

BOBBIE *(hissing) They're in his will for God's sake!*

BRICK, CECIL & KITTY *Shhhhhh!*

This is a body blow. BESS looks shaken, suddenly tearful.

We hear the organ intro to "Oh, God Our Help in Ages Past." Everyone stands except BESS.

BOBBIE *(hissing in the general direction of the coffin)* Stupid idiot!

BRICK *Shhhh!*

BRICK moves in, crouching beside BESS, who remains slumped in her chair.

Hey, hey. What's this? Come on now.

The hymn begins. BOBBIE starts to sing self-consciously, eyes lowered on her hymn book, almost mumbling.

BOBBIE "Oh God, our help in ages past, Our hope for years to come—"

BRICK *(turns his attention to BESS again, cajoling her, trying to get her to cheer up, to stand)* Hey, listen – they're playing our song.

CECIL *(joins in with BOBBIE)* "Our shelter from the stormy blast, And our eternal home."

BRICK *(to BESS)* Come on, show me that famous gumption – that famous Forrest Gumption. That's my girl—

KITTY *(joins in, singing above the others in a strong, clear voice)* "Under the shadow of Thy throne, Thy saints have dwelt secure—"

BESS reacts to this, galled.

BESS *(loud enough for KITTY to hear)* What is she? A bloody *showgirl*?

CECIL Shhhh!

KITTY "Sufficient is Thine arm alone—"

BESS *(stands, gathering herself, singing robustly)* "And our defence is sure!"

She nudges BOBBIE to start pulling her weight.

BESS & BOBBIE *(with more enthusiasm)* "O God, our help in ages past—"

They each keep raising their voices a little more, not to be outdone. By the last few lines all four are in full-throated unison. BRICK shrugs, joins in as well at the end.

ALL "Our hope for years to come, Be Thou our guard while troubles last, And our eternal *hooommme!*"

Abrupt silence. They exchange pointed glances, slightly breathless.

BRICK *(half to himself)* It's a start.

Blackout or light shift.

Scene Six – Lawyer's Office

There's a longish table centre stage now. BRICK appears, pacing, a man about to face an ordeal.

CECIL and KITTY enter and sit at one end of the table. He has a small, square package.

BESS and BOBBIE enter. Seeing CECIL and KITTY, BESS stops.

BOBBIE Look, I can do this by myself, Mum, if they make you uncomfortable.

BESS *(a bit too loudly)* Of course they make me uncomfortable!

BRICK Easy.

Hearing the raised voice, CECIL takes KITTY's hand reassuringly.

KITTY It's all right, dear. I've been through worse.

BESS I was a mayor's wife for twenty-two years, Roberta. I got through a thousand functions. This can't be worse than the Filtration Plant Prayer Breakfast. Whatever your father left them, they're welcome to it, and good riddance. And this is strictly a private matter. No one ever has to know that they even exist—

BOBBIE The lawyer—

BESS & BRICK *(together)* George?!

BESS He won't breathe a word of it. And, between you and me, I've discovered that there's precious little in Brick's account – six thousand dollars and two hundred Nortel shares—

BRICK Don't remind me—

BESS *(reacting to BOBBIE's surprise)* We always kept separate accounts. He wanted it that way. We can only guess where his money's gone. *(raising her voice, wanting CECIL and KITTY to hear)*
But if they're a couple of gold diggers expecting a windfall—

BRICK They're not—

BESS —they're in for a nasty little surprise.

KITTY *(to CECIL)* Remember, this was important to your father. Whatever he says, we accept with good grace.

CECIL Of course.

BESS and BOBBIE approach and take seats at the table, as far as possible from KITTY and CECIL.

(stands, offering his hand) I'm—

BESS Introductions aren't necessary. This isn't a garden party. Where's George?

CECIL He's given us some time alone.

BESS And whose brilliant idea was that?

CECIL Dad's. *(produces the package)* He left this. For us—

BESS For us?

CECIL —with instructions that – in the event of – if anything happened—

BRICK If I kicked the bucket.

CECIL We should look at it together, in private.

He opens the package and takes out a videotape.

So, shall I?

CECIL shoves the tape into a VCR and pokes ineffectually at the remote.

BRICK Can't change a tire to save his life.

BOBBIE For heaven's sake! Press play!

She grabs the remote, hits a button. BRICK steels himself, steps into a blue spotlight, giving the appearance that he's speaking on a TV screen.

BRICK *(intensely uncomfortable)* Well. Where's the Lagavulin when I need it?

CECIL laughs. BESS and BOBBIE shoot him a look to shut him up.

I've always hoped that none of you would ever see this tape, that I'd find the courage to face this situation while I was still alive. The fact that you're looking at it now means I didn't. I was gutless to the end, and now I'll cause pain to two people in the world dearest to me.

The others all sit staring at him, transfixed.

Before I start, I want to say to the strawberry blonde at locker twenty-seven, who looked down at a hopeless lunk lying at her feet, and thought, God knows why – I can make something of him, and did. To my dearest Bess – whose heart is as big as Lake Superior – I only hope you'll find room in there to forgive me. There are things at the end of this tape that I have to say to you and you alone, and I know the others will give us those last moments together…

And so, these are my bequests – if that's not too fancy a word, because I'm not a man to whom money meant much; although I wish I'd dumped those damn Nortel shares and bought a new truck. I was more concerned with doing the right thing, living a decent life, and I know how pathetically hollow that must ring right now…. To my darling daughter, Bobbie, the light of my life, the joy of my heart, I leave one hundred Nortel shares, my camping gear, my *old* truck, and my canoe… and my fondest wish that you'll finally find your kindred spirit. You don't even have to marry the guy, no matter what your mother says. You've proved you're hopeless at it anyway, although Bruce wasn't all *that* bad.

BOBBIE looks as if she doesn't know whether to laugh or cry.

Most of all, I hope that you'll find a way to have children of your own, so they can bring you the joy you've brought me. It's not too late, sweetheart—

BOBBIE It's *way* too late!

BRICK It's not.

BOBBIE I'm forty-seven for—

BRICK There are ways. It's a big world – beg, borrow, adopt – just do it. Because only when you hold your own child in your arms, will you truly understand that for once… once in my life I know what I'm talking about.

KITTY He's right, dear—

BOBBIE and BESS look daggers at her.

BRICK *(continuing)* To my son, *(can hardly say it)* Cecil – Sonny – who's been as good a son to me as I've been a lousy excuse for a father to him—

CECIL Not true—

BRICK —I leave one hundred Nortel shares, my service medals, my football – grab it by the laces and you'll get a nice spiral; Bobbie can show you how – and my hope that you'll find a niche in this world where your unique talents can shine.

CECIL *(shakes his head)* Unique talents—

BRICK I also hope with all my heart that you and Bobbie will become brother and sister in more than just name. The day may well come when your only family is each other, and nothing would make me happier than to have her take you rock climbing, and you take her to *The Importance of Being Earnest. (to BOBBIE)* Pick a small rock, sweetie. He'll grow on you.

CECIL's reaction is much like BOBBIE's. He doesn't know whether to laugh or cry.

To Kitty McCooey of Wapping, East London – who saved my life – and who was dealt a pretty thin hand in hers, and made the most of it with a song and a smile, and never once complained—

KITTY Not true.

BRICK —well, maybe that one time when I almost dropped Sonny off the Brighton pier – I leave my thanks, my abiding affection, and my only material possessions of any worth – my piano—

KITTY *(surprised)* Oh, Brick, really. You shouldn't have done that—

BRICK *(simultaneously)* – and my half of our inn, The Spinney.

Her words have muffled his. For a second, everything freezes.

BOBBIE & CECIL What did he say?

She hits a couple of buttons on the remote.

BRICK *(pause)* —and my half of our inn, The Spinney.

BESS & BOBBIE *What?!*

KITTY and CECIL look as surprised as they are.

BRICK I know this will come as a shock, but for years I've harboured this secret hope that the four people who mean the most to me in this world will somehow—

But BESS stands abruptly, punches off the machine, freezing BRICK in mid-sentence.

BOBBIE *(gets up to go as well, fuming.)* Thanks, Dad.

KITTY I had no idea – I – please believe me—

But BESS and BOBBIE walk away. BRICK steps out from behind the "TV screen" and goes after them.

BRICK Bess, Bobbie, please – hear me out. Listen to the rest of the tape—

But BESS just stands there, stunned. BOBBIE puts an arm around her.

BESS He said the four people who mean the most to him. He just grouped us with them, as if we're no more to him than, some – some chorus girl—

BRICK That's not how it was—

BESS —and her bastard!

She walks away.

BRICK No. *(to BOBBIE)* Sweetie, please—

But BOBBIE follows her mother off. BRICK stands there in frustration and despair unmoving.

Talk to them.

KITTY *(to CECIL)* We shouldn't have come.

CECIL doesn't notice, almost as if he hasn't heard her, staring at the TV.

Blackout.

Scene Seven – The Inn (Night)

The room is in darkness. BOBBIE comes down the stairs a bit stealthily, clicks on a light. We see that she has the videotape.

BESS is sitting in an armchair, a glass of Scotch in hand. BRICK is sitting close by, as if silently communing with BESS.

BOBBIE doesn't see BESS, goes to put the tape into the VCR.

BESS *(quietly)* What do you—

BOBBIE *(jumps, startled)* Shit! Mum?

BESS What do you think you're doing?

BOBBIE *(looking a bit guilty)* I went back and got it. I thought – I mean, don't you want to look at it? Now that we're alone?

BESS No. I don't.

BRICK *(to BOBBIE)* Just play it.

She looks tempted, but doesn't.

BESS I thought he'd have better taste, didn't you? She seems a bit – common. Probably whips up a nifty bangers and mash. And then they sit around on plastic seat covers watching telly.

BOBBIE *(avoids this topic)* What are you doing down here, Mum?

BESS Can't sleep.

BOBBIE You might have a better chance if you put down that glass and went to bed.

As if in defiance, BESS refills her glass.

BESS I lie there, the room full of his things, his clothes, his smelly old football, and my mind starts racing. Too many doubts, too many memories—

BOBBIE But good memories, surely. I mean what was that business about the hopeless lunk lying at your feet?

BESS just shrugs.

Oh, come on. Did he kneel down and propose to you, or something?

Heather Esdon and Mo Bock
photo by Tim Fort

BRICK Hardly.

BESS *(a bit reluctantly)* Hardly. He fell on his head…

BOBBIE Yes, and…?

Subtle change to "memory" lighting – and it's as if BRICK gets caught up in the memory too, becoming part of it.

BESS The boys were coming in from football practice. I was at my locker. I could see the others laughing, needling him, as if it was a dare—

BRICK It wasn't a dare. I'd had a crush on you since those piano lessons with Mrs. Davern.

BESS Suddenly he turned and came swaggering up to me—

BRICK Trembling in my boots—

BESS —and his cleats slipped on the polished floor, shot out from under him, and he landed flat on his back; gave his head the most sickening whack. If he'd had better manners, he would've taken his helmet off, and split his skull open like a watermelon—

BRICK Agh, I did it to get your sympathy. I'd heard you didn't like football players—

BESS I had no interest in a dumb football player. I had other admirers – Googie Biggs—

BRICK Googie Biggs!

BESS —but lying there, all muddy and sweaty and crimson with embarrassment, he looked—

BRICK Like an idiot.

BESS —he looked – loveable – and I think he stole my heart then and there. It certainly wasn't anything he said—

BRICK *(shaken, tongue-tied)* I was – that is – I was wondering – uh – I was going to – I mean I was thinking that if you, uh… maybe, uh… probably not, but… uh…

BESS Yes—?

BRICK Unusually fine weather we're having!

He turns away, mortified.

BESS *(pause)* Ceecil Brickley… did you want to ask me something?

BRICK *(blurts rapidly)* I don't suppose you'd like to go to the pep rally with me on Friday?

BESS I don't suppose… I wouldn't. If you don't split your skull open in the meantime.

BRICK *(breaks into a huge grin)* Oh, it's pretty thick. Okay, well, see you Friday.

He starts off, stops.

Uh – would you mind awfully not calling me – that name?

BESS What name?

BRICK You know.

BESS *(shrugs a bit mischievously)* We'll see… *(pause)* Ceecil.

He flinches visibly, a knife between the shoulder blades, as he walks away.

BOBBIE laughs as the lighting shifts back to normal. BRICK resumes a position in the background, listening.

I was in grade nine. He was in grade eleven. I drummed a few manners into him – and I never called him Ceecil again. We went together from that day on. He enlisted the day after he graduated. I took the train to Halifax and we got married three days before he shipped out. I was seventeen. He was nineteen. I never looked at another man, he never looked at another woman. Or so I thought. We were partners. Two halves of a whole. He was the host here. I was the hostess. He was the mayor. I was the mayor's wife. And he was more than just the mayor, he was Mr. Volunteer. Every committee, every fundraiser, every bingo, every chili fest, every telethon, walkathon, swimathon, bike-athon, fun-athon, *bore*-athon, he never said no to anyone—

BOBBIE Maybe he was trying to make up for something.

BESS And I never said no either. *I* should have gotten the friggin' Order of Canada!

BRICK Except you wimped out on the Polar Bear Plunge.

BESS *(points to it)* That little plaque we have over there – you know what it says?

BOBBIE Something about armour?

BESS "Let your first love be your last—

and BRICK *(saying the words quietly with her)* —and you will have put on all the armour of life."

BESS I truly believed that.

She goes over and gets it.

I thought when I fell in love with your father that I'd put on all the armour I'd ever need. But now my armour's gone, and I feel – I feel as if the whole thing, my life, has been a fraud—

BOBBIE That's not—

BESS —a sham.

BOBBIE Of course it hasn't.

BESS *(picks up a sheet of paper)* They've emailed me his Order of Canada citation to check for "inaccuracies." *(reading)* "The word hero is bandied about pretty lightly these days, but in the case of Cecil Beauregard Brickley, it fits like a glove." Blah, blah, blah. Inaccuracies! It's one big fat lie!

She crumples it and tosses it in the garbage.

BOBBIE You don't believe that.

BESS What can I believe now?! Can I believe anything he told me? Can I believe he meant it when he said he loved me?

BRICK Yes.

BOBBIE Yes. You can.

BESS Are you so sure? I was pregnant with you, you know, when he took that first November trip. I was going to wait 'til he got back to tell him. I didn't want him to worry, but I couldn't help myself. We'd been trying for six years to get me pregnant, and when he put his arms around me to say goodbye, I whispered it to him. We're going to have a baby.... That's the only reason he came back. For you. Not for me. Out of duty, out of guilt. If I hadn't told him, he would have just stayed over there. With them. He never really loved me at all.

BRICK I did—

BOBBIE Of course he did! And it's not just you! He lied to me too! Always promising to take me on that stupid canoe trip! So I'm hurt too. And royally pissed off! But you'll never hear me say he didn't love us. Because he did... he did.

BRICK I do.

BOBBIE So stop this wallowing – and crap and—

BESS Show a little gumption? Fine.

She abruptly tosses the plaque in the garbage.

There! Gumption, gumption, gumption. Your father used to say that. Such a stupid-sounding word. *Gumption.*

BOBBIE *(hands it to her)* Look at the tape, Mum.

BESS Never! What's it going to be but more lies?! How dare he do this to me? I spent my life doing as he asked, trying to please him. But it's over now, that life. This is my last chance to say no.

She dumps the tape in a wastebasket.

Gumption.

BRICK No!

BOBBIE No—

She steps forward to retrieve it.

BESS Leave it!

She finds a sudden resolve, fuelled by the Lagavulin.

Now, get those Brits in here tomorrow and we'll send them packing.

BOBBIE How?

BESS We'll do what your father said. Give them half the value of the inn.

BOBBIE But – do you have a clue what it's worth?

BESS Half a million, at least. We had a firm cash offer for that last year.

BOBBIE But how can you possibly raise $250,000?

BESS Some of us had the brains to sell our Nortel when it was at a hundred and twenty bucks.

BRICK *(impressed)* You *should've* gotten the Order of Canada.

BESS Listen, I've dealt with suppliers and building inspectors and other crooks for forty years. I can deal with a couple of wankers from Wapping—

BOBBIE *(laughing)* This is a whole new side of you, Mum.

BESS A couple of poofs from Piccadilly.

BOBBIE Just one poof, strictly speaking—

The Lagavulin and their general state of emotional and physical exhaustion has its effect, and they start to get giggly.

BESS A couple of sods from—

BOBBIE The old sod!

BESS A couple of twits from Twickenham!

BRICK shakes his head impatiently, walks off. BOBBIE and BESS are giggling foolishly now, more than this really warrants.

BOBBIE A couple of pricks from Prickenham!

BESS *(goes back to her chair, pouring another Scotch)* A couple of – a couple of – slubberdegullions!

BOBBIE *(pause)* What?

Blackout.

Scene Eight

We hear a few bars of "God Save the Queen" and the lights come up, suggesting the surreal quality of a dream. This dream-like quality of lighting is gradually heightened as the scene progresses.

KITTY is backlit, almost unrecognizable in an extravagant hat and boa.

KITTY *(a nightmarish parody of Adrienne Clarkson)* As your Governor General and de facto Queen – and high time too – it gives me regal pleasure to call upon nine-year-old Roberta Brickley to make the next presentation—

BOBBIE comes forward, her manner transforming itself into that of a girl of nine or ten, at once proud and nervous.

BESS Make your father proud, dear.

BOBBIE looks around and retrieves the crumpled Order of Canada citation from the fireplace (or wherever BESS threw it).

KITTY We're waiting. Try not to fidget.

BOBBIE The topic of my oral composition today is – My Dad, My Hero.

BESS *(confidentially, to an unseen person beside her)* I'm her mother.

BOBBIE *(smooths the paper, starts to read some big words that she doesn't always understand)* The word hero is bandied (?) about pretty lightly these days, but in the case of Cecil Beauregard Brickley, my dad, the term fits like a glove.

BESS *(to the unseen person)* She had just a smidgen of help with it.

During this, CECIL and KITTY slip into their seats, listening.

BOBBIE Enlisting at age eighteen, my dad won his wings as a bomber pilot and flew thirty-one highly dangerous missions over Germany—

BRICK strolls in, fancying himself the centre of attention. BESS pats the seat beside her, expecting him to sit with her, but he walks right by, sits down with KITTY and CECIL. They greet him with hugs and warm familiarity.

(a bit confused by this, perseveres) Wounded on his final mission, my dad spent months in hospital in England – recup – recup—?

BESS *(trying to ignore BRICK and the others)* Recuperating. Good, dear.

BOBBIE —before returning home to his beloved wife Bess, my mum—

KITTY *(stage whisper)* The old ball and chain!

BRICK chuckles, drapes his arm around KITTY.

BESS, humiliated, tries to ignore them.

BOBBIE *(getting more flustered)* My dad also served his town as mayor for twenty-two years, and was instrumental in building a new filtra – filtra—

BESS Filtration and sewage treatment plant.

BRICK Shit happens!

CECIL and BRICK laugh raucously.

BESS Please, I'm trying to listen.

BRICK, CECIL & KITTY *(mockingly)* Oh, *shhhhhhhhhh!*

CECIL The wet blanket speaks!

BOBBIE *(confused and unsettled, presses on)* An avid (?) canoeist—

CECIL Canoeist!

BRICK I enjoy the occasional paddle.

KITTY *(giggles like a schoolgirl, pokes him)* I'll say!

BOBBIE —and outdoorsman—

CECIL Out-swordsman!

BOBBIE —even at age seventy-five.

CECIL Still a bit of a lad, our dad!

BRICK guffaws. He and CECIL punch each other in the shoulder like a couple of frat buddies.

KITTY *(giggling)* Stop it, you two! You're so bad!

BRICK That's my boy! A chip off the old Brick!

BOBBIE looks baffled and upset.

BESS Never you mind, dear. Keep going.

BOBBIE A friend to all, a hero, a loving husband—

CECIL Or so the story goes!

BOBBIE —my dad. I will now present him with this extra special Order of Canada medal—

She beckons to BRICK to come up. KITTY gives him a warm congratulatory kiss and BRICK rises and strolls up, winking back at KITTY and CECIL.

BRICK Who says you can't fool all the people all the time?

CECIL Can I have your medal, Daddy?

BRICK What's mine is yours, Sonny boy. *Mi casa, su casa.*

KITTY *(sweetly, to BESS)* Your house is our house.

BRICK stands before BOBBIE, showing scant interest in her. She holds up a large Order of Canada pin.

BOBBIE I made it myself, Daddy.

CECIL Cheap! Cheap!

BRICK *(dismissively)* Yeah, yeah. Whatever. Let's get this over with.

BOBBIE looks crushed. She runs to her mother. BESS, furious, grabs the medal.

BESS I'll do it.

CECIL Wet blanket approaches!

BESS jams the pin angrily into BRICK's chest. He doesn't react. She throws it aside, slaps him across the face.

CECIL & KITTY Ooooh!

CECIL Wet blanket reveals nasty streak!

They jump up to comfort him, but BRICK shrugs it off cavalierly.

BRICK She can't hurt me. I'm dead.

CECIL Good one, Daddy!

KITTY *(kittenishly)* Come with your K-K-K-Kitty now—

CECIL Nudge, nudge!

KITTY —for some nice bangers and mash.

CECIL Wink, wink!

BOBBIE Don't you want your medal, Daddy?!

CECIL He's not Daddy, he's *deady*!

He laughs uproariously as the lighting becomes more extreme, more surreal.

Laughing, almost cackling, CECIL and KITTY lead BRICK in a bizarre skipping step, swirling nightmarishly around BOBBIE and BESS.

CECIL & KITTY *(singing raucously, to "K-K-K-Katy")* D-D-D-Deady, wonderful Deady. He's the only D-D-Dad that we adore—

BESS and BOBBIE try to stop this, but they're ignored, shuffled aside.

BOBBIE Don't be dead, Daddy!

BESS Brick? Please?

CECIL, BRICK & KITTY D-D-Daddy, b-bangers and mash-y! He's the only dead dead Dad that we adore!… D-D-D—

They skip their way off, waving like cheesy vaudevillians.

BOBBIE *Daddy!*

She runs off after them, her voice echoing eerily – "Daddy – Daddy – Daddy." Left alone, BESS collapses on the sofa.

One second blackout.

Lights back up immediately – normal nighttime lighting now. BESS is lying on the sofa, asleep, writhing, mumbling—

BESS Can't hurt him, he's dead, can't hurt him—

BRICK comes in and bends over her gently.

BRICK Easy now – wake up.

BESS *(coming half awake, dazed)* Brick?

BRICK I'm here.

BESS You're... not dead? Oh, thank God! *(spilling out)* I was having this horrible, horrible nightmare that you were dead in Leicester Square and you were having an affair with this showgirl and I stabbed you with your Order of Canada pin and—

BOBBIE *(comes down the stairs)* Mum?

BRICK *(to BOBBIE)* Shhh.

BESS Uh?

BOBBIE Who are you talking to?

BRICK is still right there, but BOBBIE can't see him. Coming fully awake now, BESS looks around, her eyes passing right over BRICK.

BESS *(stands, looking around with rising panic)* Brick?!... Brick?!

Blackout.

Scene Nine – The Inn (Day)

We begin to hear "Lilli Marlene", whistled softly. Lights come up to reveal KITTY and CECIL waiting nervously. He squeezes her hand.

CECIL It'll be fine.

But he too looks nervous, strolls around, looking at things, whistling. BRICK, sitting in the background, starts to whistle idly as well, and for a few bars father and son whistle together.

BESS and BOBBIE come down. Hearing "Lilli Marlene", BESS stops on the stairs, almost faltering.

BOBBIE Mum? Are you—?

BESS I'm fine—

She steels herself, strides into the room. BRICK stands now, watches intently.

CECIL *(trying hard to be cordial)* Good afternoon, Brickley ladies.

BESS barely nods, goes straight to a table, plunks down some documents, all business.

Have you ever thought of possibly replacing the—

BESS No.

KITTY *(blurts out, nervously)* The flowers are lovely. Do you always have so many? Or are they just because of – well…

BOBBIE They're just because of – well.

KITTY It's a shame you don't have a wedding booked or, something—

BOBBIE Yes. Next time we have a death in the family we'll try to have a bar mitzvah on standby.

BESS *(to CECIL, ignoring KITTY)* Now, our lawyer advises us that we could contest the will and undoubtedly leave you with nothing, but, out of respect for my husband's wishes—

KITTY I have no intention of taking the piano.

BESS *(ignores her)* —misguided though they may be—

KITTY Just so you know.

CECIL gives KITTY a gentle little look to be quiet. He'll handle this.

BESS I've had this agreement drawn up which states that you give up any and all claims on my husband's estate now and forever in return for a cash payment representing one half of the value of the inn… 125,000 dollars, Canadian.

KITTY catches her breath. This is a huge amount to her. CECIL is much cooler.

CECIL You said one half the value of the inn?

BESS I did. The property has recently been appraised at a quarter million.

BRICK Half a million!

BOBBIE shoots a glance at her mother. BESS avoids her look.

CECIL Really? Might I see that appraisal?

BRICK *(quietly)* Attaboy.

KITTY Cecil. Don't be rude.

CECIL I just thought it might have been a tad higher.

BESS This isn't London, Mr. McCooey. If you'd care to get your own appraisal, be my guest. It shouldn't take more than three or four weeks while you sit around, waiting, running up your motel bill – a tad.

CECIL Mmhm.

BESS Mmhm, you accept?

KITTY Mmhm.

CECIL Mmhm, I get the picture.

He paces, slightly edgy.

You know, it would really spruce this place up if you got rid of this tedious animal art and—

BRICK Hey! Those are my Batemans!

BESS Those are genuine Robert Bateman reproductions!

BOBBIE Anyway, what do you care what's hanging on our walls? Unless – unless – you're planning to—

She stops herself as the idea forms…

CECIL *(pause)* To stay.

BESS and KITTY say the next two lines together.

BESS *Stay?!*

KITTY Stay?

CECIL As Dad said.

BESS & BOBBIE He didn't say that!

CECIL Well, not to quibble, but he didn't leave us half the *value* of the inn. He left us half the inn.

BOBBIE You don't think for one second that he meant that we'd actually *share* it! Under the same roof!

CECIL I think that's exactly what he meant.

BESS *Bullshit!*

Startled, KITTY is seized with a fit of wheezing.

KITTY I'm terribly sorry, *(getting out her puffer)* I think it's the perfume from the flowers. They're lovely, but—

CECIL Come on, old luv. Sit down over here and catch your breath.

He escorts her to a chair off to one side.

KITTY What are you playing at, dear? We can't stay here. With them. It's not, it's not… thinkable. Besides, I don't have any of my things, and we've paid for our return tickets, and I have to get back to – to—

CECIL *(gently)* To what?

KITTY Please, dear – just… settle this – for me. For us.

CECIL hesitates, perhaps ready to accede.

BOBBIE *(having pulled her mother aside)* Appraised at a *quarter* million?

BESS *Shhh!* Stay indeed! It's a ploy. *(deliberately loud enough for them to hear)* They're just trying to drive the price up.

KITTY *(insulted, blurts) We are not!* What sort of people do you take us for?!

Everyone is surprised at this outburst, not least KITTY. A beat.

CECIL *(seizing the moment)* Not such horrid people, once you get to know us. And we're not just being frivolous – and I don't think Dad was, either.

BESS Must you keep calling him that?!

KITTY We're not gold diggers!

CECIL And we could be a huge help to you around here.

BESS We don't need help.

CECIL But how will you manage alone? Without him?

BOBBIE *(blurts)* I'm going to take a leave of absence from teaching and come back and help out – as long as Mum needs me.

BESS looks as surprised as anyone.

Anyway, you said you were useless at practical things.

CECIL Oh, sure. Don't ask me to chew gum and change a light bulb. But put me in the kitchen and watch out Julia Child.

BOBBIE His duck stew is the bee's knees.

CECIL *(laughs)* I've often dreamt of opening a little bistro – I've looked at your menu, and it gives new meaning to the term meat and potatoes.

BESS Meat and potatoes!?

CECIL Well, I—

BESS You presumptuous, condescending, patronizing *snob!*

She marches out, fuming – pokes her head back in.

In an hour the offer will be fifty thousand!

CECIL I'll win her over.

BOBBIE No, you won't.

CECIL *(easing BOBBIE aside, quietly)* Look, I'll lay our cards on the table. London's filthy. It's death on Kitty's asthma.

BOBBIE Please don't say you want to stay for the clean Canadian air and wide open spaces.

CECIL But it's true.

BOBBIE Agh, you want to stay because it's a good deal. It probably looks a hell of a lot better than whatever you have to go back to in London. Or whomever.

CECIL That too.

BOBBIE So what is it you actually do? Are you some sort of unemployed *actor*, or something?

She means this as an insult, but he's pleased.

CECIL I've trod the boards, betimes.

BOBBIE I knew it.

CECIL I did a year on the road in *Wind in the Willows*. But there comes a point in every man's life when the realization hits him with pristine clarity – I'm too old to be touring the provinces in a badger suit – and Toad and I were just at each other's throats by the end.

KITTY That Toad!

CECIL And I worry about Kitty when I'm away.

KITTY No need to worry about me, luv.

CECIL Well, I do. So, I lead walking tours of London now – The Oscar Wilde Walk when Alan is off. The Jack The Ripper Walk. I like to think of myself as a bit of a Renaissance man—

BOBBIE snorts.

That seems to be the standard reaction. The truth is, I've had a number of abortive careers—

BOBBIE Abortive? What's that? A fancy word for failed?

KITTY No!

CECIL At times… but this won't be a failure. We won't let it. Face it, it's like Dad said – sooner or later there'll just be the two of us.

BOBBIE Great. We'll grow old together like Marilla and Matthew. Adopt a little red-haired girl named Anne.

CECIL I'd love that.

BOBBIE It's a joke! A Canadian joke!

CECIL I'd love that.

BOBBIE Oh, stop it.

CECIL Listen, there are scads of things we could do with this place – wine tastings, sing along evenings, Oscar Wilde shows—

KITTY Oh yes! Cecil does a Lady Bracknell imitation that's—

BOBBIE To die for.

KITTY You've seen it?

CECIL She's being sarcastic, luv.

KITTY Oh. Why?

CECIL It's her nature. Come on, sis—

BOBBIE Aaaagh! That word!

CECIL It'll be fun. Kitty and I are Brits, remember. We've got those "Fawlty Towers" genes. We could have an evening of Fawlty Fun!

I'll be Basil – or no, you'd be better as Basil. You've got that misanthropic edge. I'll be Manuel, *(as Manuel)* Meester Fawlty! Meester Fawlty! Meester Fawlty!

BOBBIE You're an idiot.

CECIL Good, but try it with a British accent. Teeth clenched. *(à la John Cleese)* You're an iiiiiidiot! And then slap me on the head.

BOBBIE *(exactly the way she said it before)* You're an idiot.

She holds up the agreement.

Yes or no?

CECIL *(as Manuel)* I'm from Barthelona. I know notheeng!

BRICK bursts out laughing, as does KITTY, and even BOBBIE can't resist a hint of a smile.

(spotting this) Ah! Ah!

BOBBIE *(tries a different tack)* Look, this is ridiculous. You're an urban sophisticate.

CECIL It shows, doesn't it?

BOBBIE You'd be bored stiff here. You have no affinity for a – a backwoods B and B like this.

CECIL That's where you're wrong. I gave it its name.

KITTY And he's had a picture of it on his wall since he was a child.

BOBBIE Why?

CECIL I'd imagine what it would be like to live here, all of us together, being part of, the family.

BOBBIE Gathered around the piano at night, singing show tunes.

KITTY Lovely.

CECIL She's being sarcastic again, luv.

KITTY Oh. Well, it doesn't really become you, dear.

BOBBIE No shit. Thanks for the tip. And would you mind not calling me dear?

KITTY *(taken aback)* I meant no offence. Excuse me. I'll wait outside.

She gets up and goes out, coughing slightly.

CECIL *(sharply, the second KITTY is out the door)* Look, don't be snotty to my mother, all right!? She's an old woman, without an ounce of malice in her body. So pick on someone your own age – *dear.*

BOBBIE I can do that – dear – but do you have to call her Kitty all the time? It's really irritating.

CECIL Good. *(Silence. They glower at each other.)* Our first tiff.

BOBBIE So, what were you talking about? You gave this place its name?

He just shrugs.

BRICK Tell her.

CECIL Do you know what it means? The Spinney?

BOBBIE It means – a small woodsy area? Something like that?

CECIL If you say so.

BOBBIE Fine, don't tell me.

BRICK Tell her.

CECIL *(relents)* The first couple of years Dad came over, when I was still a child—

BOBBIE Some things haven't changed—

BRICK Whsssht!

CECIL He'd take me on an old roundabout thingy that you pushed by hand—

Shift to memory lighting again.

I called it the Spinney Wheel. First thing every morning I'd say "Daddy, Daddy, take me on the Spinney Wheel!" And we'd race to the park—

BRICK takes CECIL's hand and they run together.... There's a rolling office chair at the desk and CECIL plops down on it eagerly.

(as a six-year-old) Push, Daddy!

BRICK pushes him around in a circle. CECIL is laughing, giggling like a little kid.)

Faster, Daddy, faster! Faster! Faster! Faster!

BRICK pushes faster, until he stops, gasping.

BRICK Just let Daddy catch his—

CECIL Faster! *(gets up)* It's a wonder he didn't have a heart attack sooner than he did…

BOBBIE *(unimpressed)* Well, that's a cute story.

CECIL One day, I dragged him to the park as usual—

Back in the scene, he pulls BRICK along.

Come on, Daddy—

He stops abruptly, a crestfallen six-year-old.

Someone's on the Spinney Wheel.

BRICK *(delighted)* Aah – too bad. Try the slide—

CECIL No! Spinney Wheel! Make them go away, Daddy.

BRICK I can't just—

CECIL Yes you can!

BRICK Well, okay. We'll wish as hard as we can together, and make them go away. Come on. Close your eyes – Go away.

CECIL *(eyes closed)* Go away – go away—

BRICK Our minds have super power – say it—

CECIL Our minds have super power.

BRICK No mortal man can resist it.

CECIL No mortal man can resist it.

TOGETHER Go away. Go away – Go – away—

CECIL *(peeks through his hands, looks surprised)* Daddy, look! They're leaving! It worked!

BRICK Mmm. Told you.

CECIL *(runs to the chair)* Push me, Daddy!

BRICK Listen, Sonny, I have an idea. Since I can't be here a lot of the time—

CECIL Why not?

BRICK Just because – so if you ever have to do something that's going to be extra hard—

CECIL Or scary?

BRICK Or scary – you concentrate just like you did now – and wherever I am, I'll feel it—

CECIL How?

BRICK I just will, and I'll concentrate too, right along with you, and you'll know you're not alone. And that will help give you the super power to do whatever you have to do—

CECIL Wizard! Shouldn't we have a secret super power word?

BRICK Uh – sure – uh—

CECIL Spinney!

BRICK All right. Spinney.

CECIL And no mortal man can resist it?

BRICK You've got it, kiddo.

CECIL What's mortal man?

BRICK All of us, Sonny – all of us. But not just yet. Not just yet.

He hugs him tightly.

CECIL Push me, Daddy!

BRICK starts to push him around again.

CECIL leaves the chair and steps back into the scene with BOBBIE, as we shift back to naturalistic lighting. BRICK pushes the empty chair off to one side, remains there, watching.

And it wasn't long after he got home that he sent me a snapshot and told me he'd bought this place and named it The Spinney, and I knew it was his way of telling me he was always with me. And for years afterwards I'd ask him, "When are you going to take me to the Spinney, Daddy?" And he'd always say—

BRICK Some day, Sonny.

CECIL Some day—

BRICK I promise—

CECIL —until, eventually, I stopped asking.

BOBBIE He was always going to take me on his "canoe trip" too. Maybe that was his specialty – making promises to his kids he didn't keep.

BRICK *(affected by this)* I'm sorry. I'm sorry—

CECIL Maybe he's trying to keep one now.

Silence. She shrugs.

Somehow in death he's trying to do what he couldn't do in life – bring us together.

BRICK Yes.

BOBBIE No.

KITTY comes back in, stands listening.

CECIL But I just sense it, don't you? That he won't rest easy until the people who were closest to him are—

BOBBIE One big happy family? Uh, uh. We're not Mormons, pal. And why should I care what he wants?

KITTY Because he was your father and you loved him.

CECIL And it was his last wish.

BOBBIE Says you.

CECIL *(has an idea)* I don't just say it. I'll bet you if we look at the rest of that tape, he'll say pretty much what I've been saying. I'll bet you 125,000 dollars.

BOBBIE laughs dismissively.

I'm serious. Take the bet. If I'm wrong, we'll go. Without a penny. If I'm right, we stay. Where's the tape?

BOBBIE hesitates. BESS reappears on the landing, listening.

BOBBIE We threw it out.

CECIL *(snorts, doesn't believe her)* What's wrong, sis? Afraid I might be right?

BOBBIE You'd really walk away? With nothing?

CECIL Yes! Because this isn't about money! It's about banishing the shame and the lies and the secrecy! He had a postal box for God's sake! An anonymous number so I could write to him, send him my school reports and some little thing at Christmas, and Father's Day, and he hated it! I know he did! This is about family, about uniting his two families—

KITTY It's true.

BESS It's not true! How dare you?! Two families! He had one family – us! We are his family, not you! I am his wife, not you! This is my home, not yours! I will never share this place with you! *Never! Never!*

She marches back out.

And you're not getting the piano!

Silence.

KITTY *(quietly to BOBBIE)* We'll accept the offer—

BRICK No.

KITTY *(as CECIL starts to object)* It's for the best, dear. You sign it for us. Go on—

BRICK Don't Sonny—

CECIL *(pause, sighs)* I suppose—

He goes to the table, picks up the agreement, clearly disappointed.

BRICK Spinney. (*CECIL hesitates, takes out a pen.) Spinney—*

BOBBIE *(to CECIL)* Look, don't feel badly—

BRICK No mortal man can resist us—

BOBBIE You did everything – everything a mortal man could do.

CECIL Why did you say that?

BOBBIE I don't know.

They stand there. CECIL looks around, a slightly odd expression on his face. He shakes it off and turns back to sign the paper.

BRICK *(softly)* Spinney…

CECIL *(stops again)* He wants us to stay.

BOBBIE *(silence… finally)* I know.

Blackout.

End of Act One.

Act Two

Scene One – The Inn

Pin spot on BRICK, watching from above.

BRICK This isn't quite what I had in mind...

Lights up to reveal two reception desks, side by side, with a portable partition between them. And while there's not a literal wall, it's as if there's an unspoken dividing line between the two halves of the main room.

One half is still much as it was, although more cluttered, as if the crafts and prints that formerly filled the whole room are now crammed into one half of it. The other half is now painted a bright Provencal yellow, and features French Impressionist prints and theatrical posters – Les Miz, The Importance of Being Earnest *– a kind of theatrical/bistro theme.*

BESS and BOBBIE stand waiting by the desk on the "old" side. CECIL and KITTY stand at the other desk – so they're standing virtually side by side, smiling, waiting, ignoring each other.

But you can make this work. I know you can. God, I sound like Dr. Phil.

A car door slams.

That'll be the Armstrongs.

He moves off to the side a bit dubiously to watch what he has wrought. A bell tinkles.

BESS *(to the unseen guests)* Hello!

BOBBIE Hello!

CECIL Hello!

KITTY Hello!

BESS It's the Armstrongs!

CECIL Hello, Armstrongs!

BESS *(Glares at him to shut up. They're our clients.)* Lovely to see you. Always the first ones here every year!... Yes, it has been a long, hard winter. *(pointed glance at CECIL and KITTY)* You have no idea.... Your regular room? Well, there's been a bit of an adjustment, you see. With Brick gone, the place was just too much for me. Yes, I got your card. Thank you so much. And, well, we've had to lease out one half to – to—

BOBBIE A woman and her son, from England.

CECIL Cecil and Kitty McCooey.

BESS *(ignores him)* They turned up out of the blue and made us an offer—

BOBBIE —that we couldn't refuse.

CECIL laughs. BESS glares at him.

BESS So they actually run their side independently, and we take turns in the kitchen.... Yes, it is a bit of an odd arrangement, I suppose. So your old room, The Beaver, is actually on, well, the other side now.

BOBBIE But we have a lovely room on this side overlooking...

BESS Well, of course, if you're determined to have your old room, you'll have to check with the other management.

CECIL Which would be *nous*. Now, I suspect you're referring to the Lord Alfred Douglas suite, or the Bosie Bedroom as we call it. I've redecorated it myself in a rather amusing lavender. Have a peek. Up the stairs to your right—

The following should be rapid fire, stylized, everyone bustling about on their respective sides of the inn, catering to the unseen guests.

Bell tinkles.

BOBBIE Welcome to The Original Spinney.

Bell tinkles.

KITTY Welcome to The New Spinney.

BESS Up the stairs to your left.

CECIL Up the stairs to your right.

BESS Breakfast at eight.

KITTY Breakfast at nine.

CECIL Full English—

BESS Full Canadian—

KITTY Finnan haddie? Kippers?

CECIL Eggs *à la Suisse*?

BESS Poached, scrambled, or fried?

BOBBIE À la Brickley.

Bell tinkles.

CECIL Cucumber sandwiches on the veranda.

BESS Insect repellant on the shelf.

KITTY Old-time piano favourites in the parlour.

BOBBIE Live bait in the bucket.

Bell tinkles.

CECIL Cocktails at five.

BESS Dinner at six.

CECIL Dinner at eight.

BESS All you can eat.

KITTY Poached salmon—

CECIL *—en croute.*

BESS Prime rib.

BOBBIE Uh – *au jus*!

CECIL And perchance a post-prandial digestif?

BESS and BOBBIE look at him – huh?

Bell tinkles.

BESS Sleep tight.

CECIL Nighty night.

KITTY Don't let the bedbugs bite…

BRICK What!?

ALL *(pause, realizing what she's said)* Not that we have bedbugs at the New/Original Spinney!

Bell tinkles. Action slows to normal.

CECIL comes in, sees BESS.

CECIL Oh, Bess, sorry to be a bother, but would you have such a thing as a volleyball? We have some guests who fancy a bit of a volley.

She opens a closet and hands him a half-flat basketball and a bicycle pump.

BRICK That's a basketball!

BESS Enjoy your game.

CECIL Thanks a bunch.

BRICK Bess—

She heads off – pauses to watch. CECIL looks at the flat ball, the pump, as if he's been asked to split the atom. He tries to hold the end of the pump against the ball with one hand, pump with the other, having, of course, no effect on the ball whatsoever.

BESS They won't last through July.

She exits as BOBBIE comes in from a run, finds CECIL struggling, pumping, muttering.

CECIL Rise! Rise!

BOBBIE Pump much?

She shakes her head, goes to the closet.

CECIL Philistines! Philistines! These Canadians of yours! I offer them culture! I offer them a very unassuming little Chardonnay with a hint of oak! And they demand volleyballs! Inflated volleyballs, no less! *(he drops the ball in disgust) This is impossible!*

BOBBIE *(returns with a pin)* You put the pin thingy in the pump thingy, and then you put the pin thingy in the ball thingy – and you pumpy.

CECIL It's so nice to have a—

BOBBIE *(pumping)* Man around the house?

CECIL You said it. This is a volleyball, isn't it?

BRICK Tell him—

BOBBIE No, it's a hockey puck.

She hands it to him, reasonably inflated.

CECIL You're a peach, sis. *(jogs out, calling)* All right, fun-lovers! Are you ready to volley?!

BOBBIE smiles and goes to put the pump away.

CECIL comes back in, looking deflated…

(not amused) It's a basketball.

BOBBIE Really.

CECIL You made me look a right fool.

He flips the ball at her irritably and turns to go.

BOBBIE Sonny—

He looks at her. She's never called him this before.

I'm sorry. It was silly of me.

He shrugs, goes out. She goes to the closet, grabs a volleyball, jogs to the door.

Hey! Bro! This is a volleyball. Really.

BRICK Careful!

She throws it. We hear a sharp yelp of pain.

BOBBIE Oh. Sorry.

Bell tinkles.

KITTY Wine tasting in the gazebo.

BESS Horseshoes in the yard.

KITTY And our feature attraction – an evening with Oscar Wilde.

BRICK *(as if he'd like to stop him)* Are you sure this is—

CECIL enters with a cape and a carnation, prancing around as Oscar Wilde.

—a good idea?

KITTY sits watching at the piano, nervously supportive.

CECIL *(as Wilde)* The world was my oyster – but I used the wrong fork.

KITTY laughs, but we can tell from his reaction that no one else does.

I can resist everything – except temptation—

He waits. BRICK laughs heartily, as if willing the unseen audience to join in.

BRICK I think this is more of a Three Stooges crowd, *(eyeing the unseen guests)* no offence.

CECIL All women become like their mothers. That is their tragedy. No man does. That is his.

KITTY trills the piano, forces a laugh, as does BRICK, but clearly no one else is laughing.

(starting to sweat) I must congratulate you, ladies and gentlemen. I sense that you think almost as highly of my performance as I do myself.

KITTY trills the piano again. BESS and BOBBIE watch from the other side.

BESS They're not laughing. What a shame.

CECIL *(to an unseen guest)* You're not leaving, are you, sir? You are leaving. But really, if the lower orders, like you, don't set us a good example, what on earth is the use of you?

BESS *(goes out)* I've changed my mind. They won't make it through June.

CECIL *(starts galloping, desperate)* An English country gentleman fox-hunting – the unspeakable in pursuit of the uneatable!

BOBBIE lingers, watching. This is painful.

Even BRICK and KITTY can't manage a laugh now, just suffer along with him.

BRICK *(at BOBBIE)* Do something—

CECIL looks around, on the verge of panic.

CECIL Well, I – I—

BOBBIE You iiiiiidiotttttt!

He gapes at her, she marches over to him.

Really, Manuel! You Continental cretin!

CECIL *(stares at her for a second)* Meestair Fawlty?

BOBBIE I've told you a thousand times! Stop badgering the guests with your stuuuuupid Noel Coward imitation!

CECIL Eees Oscar Wilde, Meestair Fawlty!

BOBBIE *(whacking him on the head)* Don't contradict me you snivelling Spaniard! Bad Manuel! Bad Manuel!

CECIL Sorry, sorry! I learn! I learn!

He drops cringingly to his knees, hugging her.

I am nitwit! I know notheeeng!

Aside to the audience.

Eees Oscar Wilde!

BOBBIE gives him another mock whack on the head. KITTY laughs, relieved, does a jaunty little vaudeville thing on the piano, as if this has all been part of the act.

(to audience) Thank you. *(in a half whisper to BOBBIE)* Thank you.

BRICK Thank you.

BESS comes back in, sees CECIL and BOBBIE together. She turns away, not pleased.

Bell tinkles.

BESS Blankets in the cupboard.

KITTY Chocolates on the pillow. Our house is your house. *(sees BESS glaring at her)* I mean our *half* of our house is your half – house—

An awkward beat, she turns away to the piano.

CECIL And this evening, a special treat – no, not Oscar Wilde, sir – but Hits from the Blitz, with the Wapping Warbler herself – Kitty McCooey.

BESS, fiddling with something on the old side, snorts in disgust.

BRICK starts humming, the intro to "Lilli Marlene" – as does CECIL, almost as if he hears him, as KITTY takes her place at the piano.

KITTY *(inviting the unseen guest to join in)* I expect you know this one…. "Underneath the lantern – by the barrack gate, Darling I remember the way you used to wait—"

BOBBIE enters, and hearing them, joins in as well – so, for a moment, all (except BESS) are united in song.

KITTY, BOBBIE, CECIL & BRICK "'Twas there that you whispered tenderly, That you loved me, You'd always be, My Lilli of the lamplight—"

BESS listens for a moment, turns away. BOBBIE crosses to the old side.

(and the others) "My own Lilli Marlene—"

BOBBIE is surprised to see BESS, clearly upset.

CECIL and KITTY continue the song under the following, more softly.

BOBBIE Mum? What? It's just a song—

BESS Your dad's favourite song. Our song. He whistled it constantly. If he was away somewhere, even before I saw him, I'd hear that tune, and I'd know he was home safely—

BRICK has stopped singing and is listening to her.

It's as if they've seeped into every nook and cranny of my life, as if I have nothing of him left – just to myself – but you're right. It's just a stupid, sappy song—

BESS exits.

And off key to boot!

CECIL and KITTY hear this – off-key? They finish the verse a bit awkwardly.

Bell tinkles.

BOBBIE The Muskrat. Up the stairs to your left.

CECIL The suite of Dorian Gray. Up the stairs to your right.

KITTY comes in. She looks out a window, puts a small mat on the floor, assumes a yoga position.

BESS comes in, carrying an armload of flowers and the purple vase. She looks a bit startled to see KITTY there, (but we sense that KITTY, not surprised, may have engineered this encounter).

KITTY Hello.

BESS barely nods, starts arranging flowers in the vase.

I'm not trying to put a hex on you or anything. It's just a yoga position – "the eagle."

BESS *(continues to put flowers in the vase)* Not the Wapping Warbler?

KITTY *(ignores this)* You do yoga too, don't you? I mean, he mentioned it. Brick. He did talk about you often. He had nothing but the finest things to say about you—*(quickly)* Nothing personal, nothing private.

BESS ignores her, stuffs as many flowers as she can into the purple vase.

I've never had the money to spend on proper classes – not that I'm complaining. So I just do it in front of the telly. I expect it's not the same as real classes—

BESS pointedly sets the overflowing vase on a table as close as possible to the new side, practically in KITTY's face.

Thank you. They're very fragrant. *(coughs slightly)* It surprised me that you did yoga. I got the impression that you were much too practical for something like *(takes another position)* "the warrior." He made you sound so competent – running this place. I felt like a ditz by comparison. Do you still do it at all? Yoga?

BESS *(turning to leave)* No. I used to go to a retreat in Vermont.

KITTY Oh, I'd love to do that – I mean, how nice. But when did you find the time?

BESS The second week of November.

She walks out.

KITTY Oh… well, lovely chatting with you. I'm sorry if the song—*(but BESS is gone)* —upset you.

Wheezing slightly, KITTY takes the purple vase, moves it across to the other side of the room.

Bell tinkles.

CECIL Volleyballs? Our pleasure, luv.

BOBBIE Wine tasting? Well, sure.

CECIL A fresh batch of (yuck!) dew worms on the dock—

BESS *(a bit grimly)* And we now offer kippers.

CECIL And every Saturday it's our almost famous Fawlty Towers Frolic.

KITTY But it's sold out 'til October, I'm afraid.

CECIL Why not book for next year?

KITTY *(hesitates)* Next year?

BOBBIE Yes. Why not?

Bell tinkles.

CECIL Up the stairs to your left—

BOBBIE Up the stairs to your right—

CECIL Stairs to your left.

BOBBIE Stairs to your right.

CECIL Left.

BOBBIE Right.

BESS Left.

KITTY Right.

ALL Night, night.

Bell tinkles.

Blackout.

Scene Two — The Inn

We hear singing as lights come up on BOBBIE taking notices down from a bulletin board.

KITTY and CECIL are singing the last guests out the door to "We'll Meet Again."

KITTY & CECIL See you next year!— Bye now— Toodle-oo!—

They wave to the departing guests, as BOBBIE joins in the singing for a big finish.

Bell tinkles. They're gone. KITTY and CECIL heave big sighs, hug each other.

CECIL *(collapses on a couch)* Blimey, that was work. One season and I'm toast. How has your mother done this for forty-seven years?

BOBBIE She had help and, of course, it never used to be a musical.

She pours a Lagavulin, hands it to CECIL.

CECIL *Grazie mille, sorore.*

BOBBIE *(offering one to KITTY)* Kitty—

KITTY No. Thank you, Bobbie.

KITTY wheezes a bit, worn out.

CECIL All right, luv?

KITTY Oh, tickety boo. I think I'll take my constitutional. I won't be able to much longer – with this weather, I mean—

CECIL Careful, luv. Don't overdo it.

KITTY Oh, it's just a gentle walk up towards the Outlook and back. What is it you call it?

BOBBIE Lover's Leap.

KITTY Mmhm. I've never made it the whole way.

She stops at the door, looks at them.

I wish your father could have seen you two together.

She goes. A moment of silence.

CECIL Do you think she's lost weight?

BOBBIE She looks fine to me.

CECIL This year has been a godsend. It hasn't been easy for her, you know—

BOBBIE I thought she managed pretty well here.

CECIL No, I mean life. On earth. The old vale of tears itself.

BOBBIE *(glances outside, making sure KITTY has left)* Um—

CECIL Yes.

BOBBIE There's something I've been wondering about since, well, since the night you walked in.... *(hesitates)* When he went over there – every year – Dad – was he primarily going to see you? Or her? Or both? I mean, what was their relationship? Exactly? Or approximately – or—?

CECIL *(like a hick)* Geez, I donnow whatcher gettin' at there, sis. Whatcher talkin' about. Yer bein' awful roundy bout.

BOBBIE *(laughs)* I'm serious.

CECIL What were the – gasp – sleeping arrangements? In simple Anglo Saxon four letter words? Don't. Know. Don't want to know. On the delicate – or indelicate – topic of parental sex lives, I'm a firm believer in total ignorance. And that goes both ways.

BOBBIE If you'll pardon the expression – but it's important to me – to know the truth. You don't know what it was like in this town, to be Brick Brickley's daughter. It was as if he was Wayne Gretzky or somebody—

CECIL Who?

BOBBIE A friggin' icon – and I spent my life looking for someone who could measure up, looking for something that could match what my parents had—

CECIL Or what you thought they had.

BOBBIE *(shrugs)* My girls' soccer team won the high school championship last fall, and when the final whistle blew they dumped a huge cooler of ice water on me—

CECIL Oooooh! Nasty!

BOBBIE No, it was thrilling – but afterwards, at home, alone, all I could think was – this is it, this is my life, another twenty years of running around in little shorts, yelling at children – other people's children – when I'll never... never get to yell at my own.

CECIL What a pair we are. Me in my badger suit, you in your fetching little shorts—

BOBBIE Less fetching as the years go by, believe me. Anyway, I just wonder sometimes, how things might have been different, if I'd been smart enough to figure out that my father wasn't a paragon, just a man, like Bruce – old half a loaf himself – and all the others—

CECIL And I'm sure your taste in men isn't all that bad—

BOBBIE What would you know about taste in men? Wait, I take that back.

CECIL I met one of them, Brucie boy – at the funeral last year. Didn't I tell you?

BOBBIE You know perfectly well you didn't.

CECIL You're right. I was saving it for a warm fuzzy sib moment – like this. He didn't have a clue who I was, of course – but I'm sure we'd get along famously, doing brother-in-law thingys. Changin' the oil. Bowlin', Fishin'—

BOBBIE As long as he put the yucky worm on the nasty hook.

CECIL Goes without saying. Anyway, he kept going on about something called the Leafs? I gather that's a football club. The Toronto Mighty Leafs.

BOBBIE just rolls her eyes. He's hopeless.

But why isn't it *Leaves?* Leafs isn't grammatical. It's not a word at all. When Autumn *Leafs* turn to gold – ooh! Sets my teeth on edge –

Singing operatically.

If ever I would leaf *you,* It wouldn't be in summer – It just doesn't work. Or wait, maybe it's a whole new activity – *Love me or leaf me.*

BOBBIE Offered at better massage parlours everywhere?

CECIL You've got it – *Fifty ways to* leaf *your lover* – you could use a palm frond or Pampas grass or – gasp – a maidenhead fern!

BOBBIE *(laughing in spite of herself)* That's maiden*hair* fern.

CECIL You're so horticultural. Oh, I've got another one—

He launches into "California Dreamin'," substituting "leafs" for "leaves," encouraging BOBBIE to join in. She does, and they belt out a couple of lines together.

They realize BESS has come down the stairs and is watching. The song comes to an abrupt halt.

BOBBIE *(joins in)* All the *leafs* are brown—

TOGETHER And the sky is grey, *(belting it)* I went for a walk on a winter's *dayyyy!*

They realize BESS has come down the stairs and is watching. The song comes to an abrupt halt.

CECIL Bess! Another smashing season in the can. Let me pour you a dram to celebrate.

BESS *(very cool)* No, thank you. And this year was a breeze, Mr. McCooey. I only had half as much to do, you see. Could I speak to you, Roberta? If your number is quite finished?

CECIL Well—I was just leafing—on a jet plane.

He goes, humming to himself.

BESS If only that were true. *(to BOBBIE)* Well, I didn't realize you two had become quite such bosom pals.

BOBBIE I thought you were out.

BESS This is my home. Consider me in. At all times.

BOBBIE Anyway, we're not bosom pals. As much as you may not like it, we're brother and sister.

BESS You are not! You are *half* brother and *half* sister – if that – and he's not my half anything! There's not one drop of my blood in his veins! He's nothing to me!

BOBBIE What do you mean? If that?

BESS It's obvious. We should have demanded a DNA test. Do you see one shred of your father in him?

BOBBIE I do, actually – his spirit, the twinkle in his eye.

BESS *(hates this answer)* Fine! If you think they're so much more *spirited!* So much *twinklier!* Go on! Go over to their side! I'll run my half without your help! In fact, I'll just give it to you and disappear, and you three can have a great old time! You can start your own trio!

BOBBIE Oh, Mum—

BESS You seem to get along so much better with them than you do with me – old boring Bess—

BOBBIE For heaven's sake—

BESS Your father obviously felt the same way.

BOBBIE just sighs.

I'm going to the cemetery. It's the anniversary of his death – which you seem to have forgotten. *They've* certainly forgotten. Small wonder, what with having to remember the words to all those songs.

She goes out, very upset. BOBBIE stands there.

BOBBIE *(to herself)* I haven't forgotten.

Lights shift.

Scene Three – Cemetery

An (imaginary?) headstone, downstage centre.

KITTY stands at the grave, head lowered. BRICK stands nearby, watching.

BESS enters, holding flowers, stops in surprise at the sight of KITTY.

KITTY kneels and rests her cheek against the headstone. BESS turns away. This is painful for her to watch. BRICK puts a comforting hand on KITTY's shoulder. After a moment, as if in response, she stands and walks away.

BESS waits until she's gone, goes to the grave herself. She starts to put down her flowers – then suddenly breaks down, flinging them at the headstone, in grief and rage and confusion.

BESS Why did you do this to me?! *Why?!*

She's talking to the headstone, but it's as if her words are flung right at BRICK.

Were you so unhappy with me?! Did you hate me that much?! Is this some perverse trick you're playing on me from the grave?! Forcing them on me?! To torture me?! To punish me?! For what? For not being exciting enough? For not being a *showgirl?!*

BRICK No.

BESS I could have been different – if you'd asked me—

BRICK I didn't want you to be different.

BESS I was a singer too! A good singer! Mrs. Davern told me I had a pretty voice. I would have sung for you – if you'd asked me – but you never asked me. You never asked me—

During this we see that KITTY hasn't entirely left. She stands off to the side, watching.

(starts to sing "Lilli Marlene" haltingly, sobbing) "Underneath the lantern by the barrack gate – Darling I remember the way you used to wait—"

BRICK puts his arms around her.

(sobbing, singing) "'Twas there that you whispered tenderly—"

She breaks down and can't continue.

BRICK *(prompting her, softly)* "That you loved me—"

BESS "That you loved me—"

BRICK *(holding her)* And I did.

BESS But you didn't. You didn't.

BRICK *(to KITTY)* Tell her.

BESS You couldn't have.

KITTY stands watching this, torn. She looks as if she wants to go to BESS, to comfort her. But the moment is too private, the pain too raw.

BRICK *(to KITTY)* Please tell her.

But she doesn't move.

Blackout.

Scene Four – The Inn

Night. BESS (in a bathrobe?) goes to the liquor cabinet. As she pours herself a Lagavulin, KITTY comes downstairs behind her.... BESS turns, a bit startled to see her.

KITTY Your wee secret is safe with me.

BESS ignores her.

You've made your point, you know. You don't have to go on making it day after day after day.

BESS *(icily)* My point?

KITTY That I'm beneath notice. That I don't exist.

BESS Yes, that's my point.

She walks past KITTY towards the stairs, as if she isn't even there.

KITTY What do I have to do to make you talk to me?

BESS *(pause)* Nothing I can think of. There, we've talked.

KITTY Please—

She dashes across the room and blocks the stairs. The two women face each other, almost as if they're going to come to blows – but the quick move triggers KITTY's asthma. She starts gasping, wheezing, fighting for air.

(pointing, gasping) My puffer – my bag – under the counter—

BESS, taken aback, hurries and gets it. KITTY takes a couple of puffs, slumps down in a chair.

BESS I didn't realize you were—

KITTY *(gradually regaining her breath)* Such an old wreck? When you have me cast as the femme fatale? I'm not. I've felt so much better over here – my asthma has hardly acted up at all. There's only been one problem really—

BESS The flowers?

KITTY No. The fact that our being here is causing you such pain.

Silence. BESS doesn't respond.

He said you were stubborn, but I hoped – as time went by—

BESS What? What exactly did you hope?

KITTY —that you'd accept us – that, that we might even become friends. I've never had many friends.

BESS Well, I have – hundreds! Mind you, I haven't seen much of them lately, because I'm too humiliated.

KITTY But no one knows who we are.

BESS People aren't fools! They can put two of you and one of him together.

KITTY Cecil and I have talked it over. We can see the distress we're causing. I've decided – we've decided – to go.

BESS *(taken by surprise)* Well. Fine. And please don't assume our previous offer is still on the table.

KITTY We don't want anything from you.

BESS Very considerate, considering what you've taken already.

KITTY What have we taken?! *Nothing!* You think because he loved his son, he loved his daughter any less? You think because of me – he loved you any less? You're so wrong, about so many things. You and Bobbie were everything to him – I was just—

BESS A bit on the side?

KITTY Damn you! It must be wonderful to be so smug and quick to judge! Here in your idyllic little life!

BESS Idyllic?! This isn't just an inn! This is my *home!* My marital home for forty-six years! How do you think it feels to have it *invaded* by – by my husband's – my husband's…

KITTY Whore and her little bastard?

BESS shrugs – if the shoe fits. Silence.

(quietly) I don't expect you to care, but you have no idea what it was like in London after the war. On my own. Barely eighteen, with a colicky child to care for. A singer with asthma who couldn't work at night – I had no one to leave Cecil with.

BESS Didn't you have parents?

KITTY I never knew my dad. My mum was killed in the Blitz when I was thirteen. I was sent to my aunt's, and her husband's in Ipswich, where I'd be safe – and I was – for a while. Safe from German bombs, anyway – so I didn't have parents, no. After Cecil was born, I moved back to London and I'd wheel him to Covent Garden and sing in the street. I hated it. It hardly felt better than begging. If he was sleeping, and we were doing poorly, I'd shake him awake – make him cry. That was always good for a few extra pennies. So if you call that being a showgirl, I guess you're right.

A tiny reaction from BESS.

Eventually, I moved in with a drummer with a drinking problem. He'd come home from the pub and drum on me. One night, when Cecil was six, he jumped in and tried to stop him. He gave Cecil such a whack, I just grabbed what I could carry and walked out then and there. We spent the night huddled together in a bombed out building. At dawn, we wandered down by the Thames, ended up on Tower Bridge. He got me to lift him up on the railing so he could see better – and I stood there, exhausted, holding him, staring down at the water flowing beneath us – and it was as if I was mesmerized by it, as if it was pulling at me, whispering to me – let him go, let yourself go – it would be so easy. We'd sink gently into the muddy water. No one would miss us. No one would care. We'd be at peace.... A passerby spoke to us – just a simple good morning – but that snapped me out of it. I dragged Cecil off the bridge, scared the wits out of the poor child, and I knew then that I had to do something, anything – for his sake, if not for mine – and I could only think of one person who might possibly help us. It took me weeks to get up the nerve to send the letter—

BRICK strolls on in a pool of memory light, opening a letter.

I knew it was wrong. I knew he was married. He had no idea he had a child—

BRICK *(stares at the letter, stunned)* A son?

KITTY It would have been so easy for him just to throw my letter away, let the past stay buried. I didn't tell Cecil who he was. I just told him a nice man might be coming to visit.

BESS In November.

Memory lighting expands to include CECIL, who enters and sits downstage, waiting.

KITTY Even then I could hardly bring myself to believe it—

BRICK returns, carrying a suitcase, making a a supreme effort at cheerfulness

—'til I saw him coming along the street smiling, carrying his bag, and it was as if the darkness around me started to lift—

CECIL sits waiting, a little kid, looking up at BRICK curiously.

BRICK Hello, there.

CECIL Are you the nice man?

BRICK I hope so. What's your name, big fella?

KITTY I hadn't told him—

CECIL Cecil!

BRICK *(flinches slightly)* Well—

CECIL Cecil McCooey. I'm six!

BRICK How about if I call you – Sonny—

CECIL Okay! What should I call you?

BRICK Um – um – we'll see.

KITTY We'd moved into a tiny bed-sit by the Wapping Docks. The walls, the very air reeked of poverty. I was ashamed – ashamed to have him see how I lived, how his son was being raised – but he didn't say a word. That night, he put Cecil to bed, sat and read to him from a book he'd brought—

BRICK *(sitting with CECIL singing "Disobedience")* "James James
Morrison Morrison
Weatherby George Dupre
Took great care of his mother,
Though he was only three."

CECIL I'm six!

BRICK And you've taken great care of your mother, haven't you?

CECIL Yes! When the bad man hit her I made him stop!

Silence. BRICK looks at KITTY.

KITTY I hadn't told him about that, either.

CECIL You still didn't say what I should call you.

BRICK Well, you could call me – James James?

CECIL *(thinks)* No.

BRICK Morrison Morrison?

CECIL *(thinks)* No.

BRICK *(pause)* Daddy?

CECIL *(thinks, looks at his mother)* Okay!

BRICK *(gets up, hugs him)* Night, Sonny.

CECIL Night, Daddy.

KITTY I sat there, listening to them, tears streaming down my cheeks.

BRICK *(turns to KITTY)* Thank you for telling me. For not keeping him from me.

KITTY And I knew, just knew in my heart, from that moment on that he'd take care of us. And he did.

Lights fade down on CECIL who melts away into the shadows. BRICK steps out of the memory, remains in the background, watching BESS and KITTY.

I know you despise me, and maybe you should. I wish I could say I told him to do the right thing, to go back to you, but I was selfish. And I did everything in my power to make him stay, to start a new life with us. Everything. But he was an honourable man. He took his marriage vows seriously. We had to settle for one week a year, and the cards and letters.

BESS And cash.

KITTY Do you honestly think that made up for it?! For the goodbyes each year at the airport? His son clinging to him, begging him to stay, all of us in tears – knowing it would be fifty-one weeks before we saw him again. Don't you understand? You won. We lost. He chose you over us and it wasn't even close! Fifty-one to one. He said you had a big heart – but how big is a heart that won't settle for fifty-one to one? How big is a heart that demands fifty-two to zero?

BESS isn't quite sure what to say to this. KITTY gets up and heads for the stairs.

You'll be rid of me by Friday.

BESS *(pause)* What did he mean? When he said you saved his life?

KITTY stops, looks at her, then turns away up the stairs.

Kitty?

BRICK Kitty—

Blackout.

Scene Five – The Inn (Day)

A couple of suitcases sit by the door. Some of the pictures CECIL and KITTY put up have been taken down. The conversion back to the Original Spinney has started.

BRICK sits on a suitcases, glum, frustrated, helpless to prevent what's happening.

BOBBIE comes in, damp and breathless from a run, towels off. KITTY comes downstairs with a handbag, dressed for travel.

KITTY I wish you could have got Cecil jogging—

They both laugh – fat chance!

He has the Oscar Wilde philosophy – the only worthwhile exercise is talk.

BOBBIE And he's good at that.

KITTY Oh, he'd be good at any number of things – given the chance.

Glances at the stairs to make sure he's not listening.

But it's like his dad said – he's never quite found his niche in life – and it breaks my heart. I blame myself sometimes. I had so little to offer him growing up. At the bad times, usually just after your father left, I'd think the best thing I could do for Cecil would be to get hit by a London bus. Just step off the curb. Then Brick would take him, and he'd have a whole new life, a better one. And he would have. You know your father.

BOBBIE I thought I did.

KITTY You did – and Cecil's blossomed here, don't you think? He's a born innkeeper.

BOBBIE Must be those "Fawlty Towers" genes.

KITTY And he's an innocent party. I'm the one who's the problem. I'm the wanton homewrecker. I begged him to let me go back to London on my own, but he wouldn't hear of it. But I just wonder if – after I'm dead – if you might consider, if you could see your way clear, to asking him to stay – to come back?

BOBBIE The Marilla and Matthew scenario – look, it's a non-issue. You'll live to be a hundred.

KITTY At least. Well, the cab isn't coming for an hour. I'm going to take one last constitutional. See if I can make it all the way up to Lover's Leap for once. I'll miss those… and you.

BRICK stands, reacting to this with a hint of concern. BOBBIE says nothing, a bit embarrassed.

He's your flesh and blood, dear. It's a scarce commodity. Will you think about it?

BOBBIE hesitates – nods. KITTY starts to go, turns back and hugs her.

Sorry, I know you don't like me calling you, dear.

She goes to the door.

BOBBIE Kitty. I don't mind.

KITTY *(smiles)* Bye.

BOBBIE Oh, I'll see you before you go.

KITTY smiles at her, exits. BOBBIE goes into the kitchen. BRICK, vaguely concerned, goes out after her.

CECIL comes down, sets a last bag down by the door. BOBBIE comes back in, sipping a drink.

CECIL Sis! Cheeky monkey! Imbibing Pernod so early in the day! Have I been such a pernicious influence?

BOBBIE It's Gatorade.

She offers him a sip. He reacts in horror – a vampire to a cross. Silence, both a bit subdued.

CECIL Well.

BOBBIE Well.

CECIL Well, I was chuffed to have a sister for a while.

BOBBIE I'll still be your sister. Hey, I got along better with you than with most of my husbands.

CECIL *(hesitates)* There's one thing I've wanted to tell you. When you said that time that my relationship with Dad was just a technical thing—

BOBBIE Oh, stop reminding me! I can be a horrible, miserable, sarcastic—

CECIL *(as if to say keep going)* Mmmhmm…

BOBBIE —awful, nasty, bad person.

CECIL And sweaty.

She makes as if to shove the damp towel in his face. But the attempt at gaiety is short-lived.

Anyway, you said I was never around for the hard times, but actually, I was once.

She has no idea what he's talking about.

When dad went in for his emergency bypass surgery—

BOBBIE November '84—

CECIL I flew over and went straight to the hospital. I even gave some blood, in case he needed a transfusion. When I came into the waiting room, I saw you and your mum, crying, hugging each other, and for an awful second I thought the worst – but then I realized they were tears of joy, that Dad must be out of danger. And then I was crying too. I wanted to go to you – to cry with you, to be part of your embrace – but I couldn't. I didn't belong… but I just wanted to say, that for the time we've been here, you did make me feel as if I belonged, as if I were included in your embrace – I didn't just imagine that, did I?

She gives a little shake of her head. He didn't.

I'd always hoped I could make a big cassoulet for the four of us. That we'd all sit down together and laugh and carry on – like a family. I'm sorry your mother didn't feel the same way, but it's a lot to ask – too much to ask.

BOBBIE It's a lot to ask.

CECIL hesitates, as if he wants to say something.

What?

CECIL Nothing, just… thanks. For being a good sister to me. I couldn't have asked for a better one.

He kisses her impulsively, picks up his bags and goes to the door.

BOBBIE Neither could I.

He stops, looks back at her, oddly solemn.

It was a joke!

CECIL I know. It was funny.

But he seems hesitant, visibly emotional.

BOBBIE Stop that! This isn't "Casablanca"! Some big, sad goodbye! I'm coming over in the spring. You'll buy me lattes and take me on The Oscar Wilde Walk. It's a date – or whatever – with my brother.

CECIL *(pause)* Or whatever.

BOBBIE What's that supposed to mean?

CECIL At the hospital, when I was leaving—

BESS comes in, looks disconcerted to see him.

BESS Oh. I thought you'd left.

CECIL Forgotten but not gone.

BESS Well, have a nice flight.

She waits, expecting him to leave. An awkward beat. It's harder now with BESS listening.

CECIL *(to BOBBIE)* At the hospital, when I was leaving—

BESS turns to go.

No, stay. You have a right to hear this too.

BOBBIE *(to BESS)* He came over for Dad's bypass.

CECIL I asked if they'd needed my blood, and they told me no. In fact, it wasn't a match. Mine was A and Dad's was O. A father and son don't necessarily have the same blood type – but it was like a tiny cloud in the back of my mind – and finally I asked Kitty if she knew what blood type she was, and she said, oh yes, she used to give blood all the time during the war – type O. Well, you don't have to be Bloody Mary – little blood joke there – to know that two O's don't make an A. I'm sure Mum honestly believed I was his son. I had to be. It was the only thing that made her life bearable. I never told Dad, never said anything to either of them, because I wanted him to keep coming – and he did, every November, because we needed him. Because that's the kind of man he was.

To BESS, with a hint of bitterness.

I know you've decided he was a liar and a hypocrite, but you never even had the decency – or the nerve – to listen to his side of the story. So you had it tabbed all along, Bess. I'm nothing to you. Not even technically. So you needn't feel any obligation – or guilt. You needn't feel anything at all.

To BOBBIE.

Sorry, but I couldn't just walk away and leave you with the lie.

Goes to the door and takes a last look around.

You should think about changing the name of this place. Spinney – it's a childish word, really. And no one knows what it means.

He goes out.

BOBBIE *(to herself)* Except us.

She steps forward, as if going after him.

BESS Let him go. It's over.

BOBBIE It's not over.

She goes off (although not after CECIL).

BESS turns away and starts to take down CECIL's posters from the new side.

Downstage (or in front of the stage) KITTY walks across purposefully, her breathing laboured.

BOBBIE re-enters, holding the video. BESS pays no attention as BOBBIE puts it in the VCR.

BRICK re-appears, steps into a special light (again suggestive of a TV screen) as she starts the tape.

BRICK —for years I've harboured the secret hope that the four people who mean the most to me in this world will somehow—

BESS turns, startled by the sound of BRICK's voice, almost as if she doesn't know where it's coming from. She stares at BOBBIE, at the TV.

BESS You kept it?

BRICK —will somehow find a way to – to—

He stops, at a loss for words, tries to gather himself.

BESS still can't bear to hear this, turns away.

BOBBIE *(takes her hand)* Look at it, Mum.

BRICK Oh God, Bess, I wanted to tell you. And I did – countless times.

BESS turns back – what is he talking about?

I'd lie in bed, wide awake, with you asleep beside me, and I'd whisper it to you – the whole story—

BESS doesn't move, stares at the screen.

—and I had this foolish hope that one of those nights you'd turn and say – "I wasn't asleep. I heard every word – and it's all right – you're an idiot, but it's all right". But would you have? Or would our whole life have come crashing down?

BESS I don't know—

As he continues, she slowly crosses the room and sits close to the TV – listening.

BRICK I'll never know. And so, to you, the strawberry blonde at locker twenty-seven – my first love and my last – I leave my wedding band, my unfinished life, and my story, the one I whispered to you, in the night—

BOBBIE turns to leave. This is private.

BESS No. Stay—

BRICK Every time you fly a bomber, you're this big, fat, slow, juicy target. And you know the German fighters are out there. You can't see them, but they're out there in the night, out there to kill you. And sooner or later they will. It's a cosmic certainty.... We'd had three rough trips in a row – limped back to the base, pretty badly shot up. I had the shakes. Couldn't keep any food down, was desperate, desperate for a few hours sleep.

BOBBIE takes her mother's hand, and they sit watching together.

I went to the doc, didn't tell the boys. He gave me a couple of blue pills, a bed in the infirmary. And he offered to take me off the battle order for twenty-four hours. The weather was socked in. I was sure there wouldn't be any bombing runs that night, so I said okay. When I woke up that evening, the weather had cleared. The sky was a perfect blue. I still had time to get to the briefing, but I didn't go. And my crew, Brickley's crew, took an eight-hour bombing run to Berlin with a spare pilot, while I lay there snug in my bed, pretending to sleep…. We lost nineteen planes that night. But my boys made it back. When I saw them coming in at dawn, I said a prayer for the only time in my life, I thanked God, and went out to meet them, almost too ashamed to face them, ashamed that I'd let them go without me. They touched down, blew a tire – and smashed head on into a Lancaster with a twelve thousand pounder on board. You could have heard the explosion in Leicester Square. I ran across the tarmac, grabbing at the flaming wreckage with my bare hands, trying to get to my boys. They were my family, closer to me than brothers. But it was a cauldron, it was hopeless. They had to drag me away. They should have charged me with Lack of Moral Fibre, cut the buttons off me, drummed me out like a dog. Instead, they stuck me in the hospital at Ipswich on a suicide watch. For fifty years I've let you think I was wounded, but that was just another lie. I wasn't wounded. I wasn't suicidal, either. I was just waiting for my hands to get better. Then I'd fly again. I'd die honourably. I'd redeem myself.

CECIL *(comes back in)* I—

Riveted by BRICK, BESS hardly notices him.

BOBBIE Shhh—

She beckons him in and he remains, watching.

BRICK Once a week this girl, she didn't look more than seventeen, would come out to the hospital and sing for us. She sang like an angel – a sad angel.

We hear KITTY, off, singing "(There'll Be Bluebirds Over) The White Cliffs of Dover".

She continues softly under.

I got roped into playing the piano for her – after a fashion. The doc said it would be good therapy for my hands. One afternoon, she was singing, and suddenly Churchill was on the radio, the Germans had surrendered. The war was over. People went crazy, kissing everyone in sight. But for me, it was like a kick in the stomach. My chance to fly again was gone. I'd have to live with what I'd done. Forever.

Shift to memory lighting as he walks.

It was easy to walk away. I went out to the cliffs overlooking the estuary—

He stops downstage, looks down, as if over a cliff.

It was as if I was already a dead man. I just had to punch my ticket.

He steps forward to the edge of the cliff. KITTY appears behind him.

KITTY Cheer up, luv. The war's over.

He turns, startled – what's she doing here?

I followed you.

BRICK Why?

KITTY Why? For an apology, that's why. There I am, smack in the middle of my big number, singin' me knickers off, and my piano player ups and walks out without a fare thee well. If I were a sensitive gal, I might be right insulted.

BRICK I thought the song was finished—

KITTY Not only that, but I find you about to hop, skip and skeedaddle off a bleedin' cliff!

BRICK I – I wasn't going to—

KITTY And I was in *good* voice today. I hate to think what you'd be up to now if I'd been off key!

BRICK *(almost laughs)* It had nothing to do with—

KITTY *(has a horrible thought)* Blimey!

BRICK What?

KITTY I wonder if I'm liable. Criminally negligible singing causing gross bodily harm.

BRICK *(starts to laugh)* I realized I hadn't laughed in months – I think it's negligent—

KITTY I'll say! I can just see your wife and poor wee kidlings weeping in front of the judge. Her singing was so egregious, your lordship – they use big words like that – she drove our poor dad to leap off a cliff and smash his gob on—

She looks over the edge.

—ooh – on some nasty bloody rocks – poor little lambs who've lost their da – baah, baah, baah.

BRICK *(laughing)* I don't have any… little lambs.

KITTY Or a poor little wife?

BRICK *(tiny pause)* No… I was shocked by how easy it was. To lie.

KITTY So you won't mind if I join you then?

BRICK Join me?

KITTY I'm obviously a menace to society, driving grown men to suicide. Come on. Take my hand. We'll jump together—

She takes his hand, steps forward. Laughing, he pulls her back.

BRICK Stop it!

KITTY No?

BRICK No.

KITTY So. What then?

BRICK Well, can I walk you home?

KITTY *(laughs bitterly)* Home. I don't have a home. I had a room, with my aunt, and her husband, but I'm not going back there. Ever again.

BRICK Why not?

KITTY *(doesn't want to talk about it)* My door doesn't lock. Come on—

She takes his hand, singing "(There'll Be Bluebirds Over) The White Cliffs of Dover" to herself, while enticing BRICK not to jump.

—Don't you be thinking about jumping now—come on.

BRICK joins in, singing hesitantly. KITTY continues humming the song softly under the following:

BRICK And so it started, I won't insult you, or her, by pretending it didn't mean anything. For those few weeks it meant everything. She made me laugh. She saved me. She healed me. I didn't tell her the truth about you until we were standing on the pier the morning my ship sailed. I was expecting an awful scene, but all she said was—

KITTY I know—

BRICK You know?

KITTY You're an egregious liar, luv.

BRICK Of course, I became a pretty slick one, with practice.

KITTY *(hesitates, as if she's going to tell him something – but she doesn't)* Have yourself a life now.

She walks away, almost makes it off before she breaks down, breaks into a run.

BRICK And I did – we did – and I wouldn't have traded it for the world. But without her, you and I wouldn't have had anything – our inn, our daughter, our life together – and when I got her letter, all I could think was I curled up in my bed and turned my back on some fellows once. I couldn't do the same to her, to my son—

Pause, revert to more conventional lighting as he moves back to his spot on the "TV screen."

So, my last request to you, dearest Bess, is that you'll find it in your heart to understand, to accept them. Both of them. And one last thing – if Sonny offers you that duck stew of his, please tell him it's pretty darn tasty—

CECIL *(nonplussed)* Which it is.

BRICK —which it is.

He makes a tiny farewell gesture as the tape ends and he steps out of the spotlight.

CECIL The cab is here—

BESS looks a bit startled, almost as if she hadn't known he was there.

I can't find Kitty.

BOBBIE She took one of her constitutionals.

CECIL Where? She knows we have a train to catch.

BOBBIE Up towards the Outlook. But she should be back by now.

BESS The Outlook? Lover's Leap—?

A beat.... Somehow it's as if they twig to this, feel a sense of alarm, all at once—

BRICK Go – go!

BOBBIE dashes out, the others right behind her.

Lights sweep across the stage dramatically, giving a sense of people running, covering ground. A nightmarish quality, although this is no dream.

BOBBIE and CECIL appear, running, BOBBIE in front. CECIL, no runner, struggling to keep up.

BOBBIE *(furious with herself)* I'm so stupid! She practically told me what she was going to do!

CECIL *(gasping, falling behind)* Never—

BOBBIE Practically spelled it out for me!

CECIL Never mind! You go ahead – Hurry!—

She runs ahead, and then off. He follows.

CECIL & BOBBIE *(shouting, off)* Kitty! Kitty! Kitty!

After a moment, BESS passes through, dragging her feet, unable to keep up.

Scene Six – The Outlook

Lighting becomes more normal as BOBBIE runs in, puffing, arriving at the Outlook. (The stage is built up to suggest the edge of a cliff.)

BOBBIE Kitty?

Worried, she looks over the edge.... CECIL comes staggering up, gasping, in a state.

CECIL Is she—?

BOBBIE No. There's no sign of her.

He's doubled over, hyperventilating.

We've gotta get you on an exercise program, bud.

CECIL But – but where is she then?! Why didn't we pass her?!

BOBBIE There are a couple of side paths. Catch your breath. We'll find her.

CECIL *(glances over the edge) What's that?!*

He's pointing down. BOBBIE rushes to the edge.

There! Floating in the water!

BOBBIE I don't know. It could be—

CECIL Her coat! Oh, Jesus! What was she wearing?!

Calling down.

Kitty! Kitty! She's not moving!

He's getting dangerously close to the edge.

BOBBIE *(grabs him)* Calm down! I'll run back and get my gear! Promise me you won't try to climb down there!

CECIL But—

BOBBIE Listen to me! I don't want to lose you too!

CECIL Why do you care?!

BOBBIE Because you're my brother, you idiot!

CECIL But I told you, I'm not—

BOBBIE Which word don't you understand?! Brother or idiot?!

CECIL *(quietly)* Brother.

BOBBIE You're his son. You're my brother. And it has nothing to do with blood types. It has to do with – with Spinney Wheels. And

I can't run that damn inn if you break your damn neck! So promise me you'll stay right there! Promise me!

CECIL I promise.

She dashes off. He stays by the brink, looking down anxiously.

Lights shift to a path below the Outlook (downstage playing area).

BESS staggers in. Unable to continue, she flops down, gasping, breathless.

She hears a faint wheezing, and is surprised to see KITTY, sitting off to the side, also struggling to catch her breath.

KITTY Out for a stroll—?

BESS *(still breathless)* We were afraid – afraid – you were going to—

KITTY Miss the train?

BESS Jump—

KITTY Jump?

BESS Jump!

KITTY Jump!?

BESS Off Lover's Leap!

KITTY *(making light of it)* That's the daftest thing I've ever heard!

BESS *(looks at her pointedly)* It's daft, all right.

KITTY All I want to do is make it to the top just once – see the view. Well, I'm off—

She stands to go.

BESS *(pause)* I looked at the tape—

KITTY stops, looks at her.

Thank you. For saving his life. For sending him back to me.

KITTY He had a lot to live for.

BESS Like you.

KITTY *(pause, quietly)* Not really, luv. Not really.

She turns to go again. BESS stands.

Please. Don't follow me. Just let me go. It's for the best. For Cecil, for everyone. Bye Bess.

She starts to walk away.

BESS He won't thank you for this. He'll hate you.

This seems to shake KITTY. She stops.

KITTY Hate me? But—

BESS And it won't work. Do you honestly think he'll want to stay here? For one minute? At the place where his mother—

KITTY's breathing is suddenly more laboured. We can see her resolve sag, her sense of defeat almost palpable.

KITTY I just – I just – don't know what else to do—

BESS I've felt the same way.

KITTY *(surprised)* You? When?

BESS The day I found out about you—

Silence… more casually.

You know, I always loved hiking, but I couldn't get Brick to walk around the block. Did he—?

KITTY Brick?! Go hiking? With me? Not bloody likely! No, no, Cecil would take me. The Cotswold Way. The Yorkshire Dales. We used to walk for miles. The idea that I can't climb a piddling little hill now just – just pisses me off! I hate being such an old crock! Hate it!

BESS Me too. So, why don't we go?

KITTY looks at her – go?

Up to the Outlook. You and I. It's a lovely view. Or was. I haven't been up there myself in years. What do you say? A summit attempt. By two old crocks.

KITTY You mean—?

BESS The war's over. And I wouldn't mind a bit of company – along the way. *(holds out her hand)* Kitty?

KITTY hesitates, in a turmoil, as this sinks in. Finally, she reaches out, takes BESS's hand.

KITTY You won't say anything? To anyone?

BESS What's to say? Two old biddies took a hike! That's news?

KITTY laughs. They take a few steps, stop and look up, way up, at where they have to go.

(and KITTY?) Oh, shit!

KITTY *(takes a hit from her puffer)* One for the road.

She offers it to BESS.

Go on, try it. It's not marijuana.

BESS eyes it dubiously.

Just press down – breathe in deeply—

BESS *(does so, holds it)* Mmmmmmm… I could get used to that!

KITTY Lover's Leap or bust!

And laughing, arm in arm, they start to walk.

(BESS joining in) I think we can, I think we can, I think we can—

They break into song.

If he could see us now! That little man of mine!

They exit as the lights shift back to CECIL. Unable to stand it any longer, he gingerly eases himself over the cliff edge… promptly slips.

CECIL Oh, shit! *(clings precariously by his fingertips) Help!*

Suddenly BRICK is there, above him.

BRICK Hold on!

But this has no effect. Desperate, BRICK drops to the ground, whispers right in his ear.

No mortal man can resist us—

CECIL *(a beat)* Daddy?

BRICK Hang on!

Matthew Gibson, Mo Bock and Tracey Ferencz
photo by Tim Fort

CECIL Where are you?! I can't see you!

BRICK That's a good thing.

CECIL I'm slipping!

BRICK Hold on, son!

CECIL But – but I'm not your son!

BRICK Never say that! Never!

CECIL But our blood didn't—

BRICK Blood shmud!

CECIL You *know?!*

BRICK I know!

CECIL But all those years? Why did you keep coming?

BRICK To see you! Because I loved you!

CECIL Like a son?

Heather Esdon and Meg Walter
photo by Tim Fort

BRICK No. As my son.

CECIL *(clinging, straining)* Not to quibble, Dad, but in that context don't "like" and "as" mean essentially the—

BRICK God you're a difficult child!

CECIL Sorry.

Lights shift to KITTY and BESS as they re-enter, singing.

BESS & KITTY We're eatin' fancy food and drinkin' fancy wine—

BOBBIE dashes in, screeches to a halt at the sight of BESS and KITTY arm in arm.

BOBBIE Mum? Kitty?

BESS We're heading for the summit.

KITTY Where's Cecil?

They look at each other.

Lights shift to CECIL, clinging.

CECIL Help!

BRICK Sonny!

BOBBIE, BESS and KITTY stop abruptly. They look up, unsettled – as if they've somehow heard this, sensed it…

BOBBIE Dad?

BESS & KITTY *(almost together)* Brick?

BRICK Pull!

CECIL *(weakening, about to lose his grip)* I can't!

BRICK *(thinking desperately)* I lied.

CECIL Uh—?

BRICK I hated that duck stew.

CECIL What?!

BRICK Foul tasting slop!

CECIL Slop!

Outraged, he gets a surge of adrenaline – manages to pull himself part way up.

BRICK Pig swill—

CECIL Pig swill!

He pulls – he's almost up – but his hand slips and he lurches sickeningly backwards.

Daddy!

BRICK *(leaning close to CECIL, willing him.)* Spinney – *Spinney*—

CECIL hangs there, clinging desperately.

BOBBIE, BESS & KITTY *(as one, as if in prayer)* Spinney…

Blackout.

Scene Seven

A beat, then we hear the strains of "Oh, Canada". A pin spot comes up on BOBBIE.

BOBBIE *(self-conscious, somewhat emotional)* Happy Canada Day, everyone – thanks for coming…

Lights up. We see that she's standing at a small podium, downstage. There's a ceremonial red ribbon loosely draped beside it. BRICK stands behind her, watching.

It's hard to believe, but it's four years now since Dad died – and I hoped my mum would do this. But after her retirement, she became a regular world traveller, gallivanting off on yoga retreats and walking tours, usually with her friend Kitty. She was supposed to be back from her latest jaunt today—

She looks around.

—but she hasn't turned up, so you're stuck with me for this official opening of the Brick Brickley Memorial Park – and water fountain, here on the grounds of the sewage treatment plant, which he worked so hard to get built. He'd be particularly glad to see the playground, and the little roundabout over there, because Dad loved kids. I think he'd have liked to have had about ten of them, instead of just – well – the number he had—

She sees BESS walk in.

There she is. I'm making a hash of it, Mum.

BOBBIE beckons to her, but BESS motions for BOBBIE to carry on.

BESS Better you than me, dear. Show a little – you know.

BOBBIE Gumption. Sure, well, over these years, thanks to a certain person—

She glances to the side – where CECIL enters now, watching. KITTY also appears, and stands watching.

—I've become familiar with Oscar Wilde. He's the man who said that children begin by loving their parents, as they grow older they judge them, and sometimes, sometimes, they forgive them. Well, today, I forgive my dad as he'd forgive me for this fumbling attempt at a speech, and still be proud of me. Because that's what families are for. For accepting us, and loving us and forgiving us. Warts and fibs and divorces and missed canoe trips and blood types and all. And so I know, without a doubt, of all the things I've ever done, my dad would be proudest of what I'm going to do now—

She goes and whispers something to BESS – BRICK stands in anticipation.

BESS No.

BOBBIE But—

BESS I'll do it—

She steps forward, gathering herself.

Lovely to see you all – Marge, George, Googie – I'd like to call on someone you've come to know – as a gourmet cook, a wine – well, not a snob exactly—

BOBBIE *(sotto voce)* A snob—

BESS —a – connoisseur – a friend – Cecil – Sonny McCooey. *(pause)* Brick's son—

BOBBIE My brother.

BESS Yes, you heard us correctly – to cut the ribbon in his father's name.

BOBBIE takes out a huge pair of scissors from behind the podium and moves toward CECIL.

CECIL *(completely taken by surprise)* No, no—

BOBBIE Shhhh! Get over here!

She gives him the scissors, steers him firmly towards the podium. CECIL smiles a bit foolishly at the audience.

KITTY, surprised as well, watches emotionally.

CECIL Well – it's permissible to be gobsmacked – I, uh—

He looks at BOBBIE, at a loss for words – help!

BOBBIE Just ease into it.

CECIL Right. Well, the one thing I wish is that – is that Kitty, my mum, had lived to see this day… but she had three wonderful years here, thanks to Bess and Bobbie – and, of course, little Soo Li, which were

Heather Esdon, Matthew Gibson, Meg Walter, Tracey Ferencz and Mo Bock
photo by Tim Fort

like a bonus for her – and, well, I just get the feeling, somehow, that she knows about this—

He looks up at the heavens.

KITTY *(to BRICK)* Why do they always look up?

BRICK Ah, what do they know, they're alive.

CECIL *(getting choked up)* Sorry, sad ribbon cuttings always make me cry. Say, how about those Leafs, uh? But why isn't it Leaves? I mean Leafs isn't even a proper word—

BRICK Okay. Cut!

BOBBIE shushes at CECIL, draws a finger across her throat.

CECIL Cut? *(makes a scissoring motion)* —and cut – I get it. So, well, *sans* further blather, *sans* further blubber – I herewith declare open the Cecil Beauregard "Brick" Brickley Memorial Park – and Spinney Wheel.

He tries to manipulate the big scissors, but they just chew at the ribbon ineffectually.

BRICK Can't cut a ribbon to save his life.

CECIL *(as Manuel)* Sorreee, sorreee! I am witnit!

BOBBIE grabs the ribbon, pulls it taut.

I know notheeeng!

The scissors slice through the ribbon. The others applaud. CECIL raises the scissors in triumph, almost whacking BOBBIE with them. She ducks, then gives him a hug.

BRICK A difficult child.

BOBBIE and CECIL beckon to BESS who joins the embrace.

BESS *(to the audience)* Now, you're all invited back to the Spinney for a big Brickley feast!

CECIL *Cassoulet du canard!*

Hearing a dubious reaction.

Duck stew!

Another groan.

Oh, all right – hamburgers.

Under his breath.

Philistines.

A piano starts to play softly – "Tipperary".

BOBBIE *(beckoning as if to a child to join the embrace)* Soo Li, sweetie. Come on… no?

CECIL Look, she wants to go on the Spinney Wheel.

BOBBIE Okay. I guess no one will object if Brick Brickley's granddaughter takes the first ride.

CECIL Go ahead, Soo Li. Uncle Sonny will come and push you.

BOBBIE We all will. Come on, Nana.

Lighting becomes stylized, starting to revolve, suggesting a merry-go-round.

They all start to move, forming a circle in sync with the revolving lights, as if stepping onto a merry-go-round.

KITTY "It's a long way to Tipperary—"

ALL *(joining in)* "It's a long way to go—"

They keep turning jauntily, joyfully, enjoying the song, enjoying the ride, enjoying each other's company and, if the mood is right, inviting the audience to join in as well.

"It's a long way to Tipperary,
To the sweetest girl I know!
Goodbye, Piccadilly,
Farewell, Leicester Square!
It's a long, long way to Tipperary,
But my heart's right there…"

They all reach out to take Soo Li's hand.

"But my heart's right here."

Blackout.

The End.

Rope's End

Introduction

"Marisa please find me
I'm almost forty-seven"

This variation on a Leonard Cohen quote has been tacked up on my bulletin board for years, serving as both an epigraph for *Rope's End* and an ever present goad to make me write the damn thing. Some day.

I don't remember when the idea for *Rope's End* first came to me; it's lurked in my psyche and in fragmentary notes for eons. Originally imagined as a short story, I still have the first two yellowing pages, typed on an old Olivetti manual, with the rather literal title, *The 20 Year Appointment.* At some point I scribbled in the margin – "good idea" – and now and then I'd come back to it, have a crack at it, put it aside, until finally I was ready to write it.

The central "good idea" of *Rope's End* is this: that somewhere in this vale of tears, somewhere on the road not taken, is the perfect person for each of us. Often we imagine this to be someone from the distant past, childhood even, long gone, but lingering in some idealized, unreliable corner of memory. A hopeless romantic fantasy, perhaps, but a pretty universal one.

Rope's End poses the question – what would happen if a man were to throw common sense to the wind and set out to put the fantasy to the test – to find that perfect person from many years before? In this Internet age, it's much easier to actually do this than in the past. We're all out there lurking, findable, in the ether. But what if she doesn't remember him? Even worse, what if she does?

Like many writers, I've had a somewhat ambivalent relationship with critics, and I've long been partial to Theodore Roosevelt's maxim – "It is not the critic who counts.... The credit belongs to the man who is actually in the arena, whose... place shall never be with those timid and cold souls who know neither victory nor defeat." But, oddly enough, I chose to make the play's central character, Toby Boone, a critic. And rather than treating him as an easy target – a figure of fun, or an object of vitriol – he actually evolved into (I hope) a highly sympathetic figure. I'm not quite sure how this came to pass. It may simply show that I'm going soft and sentimental, or, as Toby says in the play, that aliens came down at night and trampled my brain and made me do foolish things.

So is *Rope's End* a comedy? A drama? A bit of both probably. Perhaps that's how I see life – that it's neither one nor the other. Alan Ayckbourn's first rule of playwriting is; "Never look down on comedy – it's an essential part of any play. Without light how can we create shadow" – which may simply be a highfalutin way of saying "make 'em laugh, make 'em cry." So if it's good enough for Sir Alan…

In that vein, *Rope's End* is undoubtedly the first play to feature Alex Trebek and Helena Bonham Carter's rear end. Shadow and light. Make 'em laugh, make 'em cry.

Douglas Bowie
September 2007

"It is not the critic who counts, not the man who points out how… the doer of deeds could have done better. The credit belongs to the man who is actually in the arena… who strives valiantly, who errs and comes up short again and again… who knows the great enthusiasms, the great devotions, who spends himself for a worthy cause… so that his place shall never be with those cold and timid souls who know neither victory nor defeat."

—Theodore Roosevelt

Rope's End was first performed at the Thousand Islands Playhouse, Gananoque, on September 1, 2006 with the following company:

Toby Boone	Murray Furrow
Marisa/Zoe	Jan Alexandra Smith
Artistic Director	Greg Wanless
Director	D. Michael Dobbin
Set and Costumes	Arthur Penson
Lighting	David Magladry
Stage Manager	Kirsti Bruce

Characters

TOBY BOONE
MARISA/ZOE

Acknowledgements

Rope's End was rewritten extensively (and, I think, improved) after I had a chance to hear it in workshop, and I'd like to thank the generous performers who participated in this process, offered suggestions, and contributed to the development of the final play: Matthew Gibson, Kathryn MacKay, Mo Bock, Hollie Stewart and Ian D. Clark. The play continued to evolve during rehearsal, as director D. Michael Dobbin and actors Murray Furrow and Jan Alexandra Smith added their own distinctive colours in making it their own and bringing it to life for the first time.

I also gratefully acknowledge the assistance of the Ontario Arts Council's Playwright in Residence program, Alison Bowie who spent many hours helping to prepare the manuscript and Kirsti Bruce, a continuing source of positive energy throughout both *Goodbye, Piccadilly* and *Rope's End.*

And again, my particular thanks to Greg Wanless, artistic director at the Thousand Islands Playhouse, who put his support behind *Rope's End* back when it was just a rough draft of an incomplete first act, and maintained his unwavering faith in it right through to opening night.

Pre Show

As the audience is entering, we hear children's voices singing fragments of campfire songs – "Kumbayah," "Michael Rowed the Boat Ashore," "500 Miles…"

Act One

Scene One

The last song swells up for a moment – and then fades out.

Lights up on TOBIAS BOONE. He's forty-five-ish, not quite shabby, but a bit soft and nondescript – a man who could use some sunshine and exercise and a Tommy Hilfiger shirt or two.

He sits on a chair downstage in front of a scrim. The stage is basically bare – a chair, a table with a laptop, an old "Citizen Kane" poster, perhaps a couple of empty pizza boxes on the floor. TOBY takes a long slug from a bottle of beer, probably not his first of the day. It may have loosened his tongue a bit, but he's not drunk.

He's trying to tie a knot in a length of rope, talking more or less to himself, but including the audience as well.

TOBY *(making a loop with the rope)* And so we have a lake, or a kidney-shaped pool, or the fetid swamp of my imagination… and then a snake, with all of its biblical connotations, pokes its snout – or whatever snakes have – noses? probosci? – up out of the lake, slithers sinuously around the limp pizzle… and does a forward two and a half back into the pool like a veritable Greg Louganis, and voila, a perfect—

He pulls the rope taut.

—clove hitch.

But he ends up with no knot at all, just a straight piece of rope.

Turn in your grave, Lord Baden Powell. No problem—

He gets up and goes to one side.

I have just the thing, just the ticket for the clove-hitch challenged male, if I can put my hands on it—

He returns with an old shoe box.

—a shoe box, you say – but not just any shoe box – my magic shoe box, My Wonder Years shoe box—

Removes the top and smells.

—the unmistakable aroma, redolent of my childhood in all its musty banality.

He pulls out a large chestnut on a string.

My chestnut – Attila the Hun.

He hacks the desk with it, continues to pull things out.

My sharp stick—

He takes out an old 45 record.

Lorne Greene sings the theme from "Bonanza"—

He hums a few bars as he pulls out other stuff.

—my beanie decorated with miniature toilet seats.

He takes out a small, round object.

The skull of my dead hamster, Hammy. Alas, poor Hammy, I knew you well—

He continues to take things out.

A broken buzzer from my junior "Jeopardy" game… my dried and shrivelled lump of something…. And yes, my little cub hat.

He puts it on – it's several sizes too small.

You'll dyb dyb dyb! We'll dob dob – and all that crap. And here it is – before Google, before Yahoo, before the twenty-four hour Poker Channel, there was – *The Boy Scout Handbook* and *Wolf Cub's Handbook.* A fount of subversive information.

Reading.

This is to certify that I, Toby Boone, am a – *cud*? And I was always told I was a bright child—

Reading.

Weight – fifty-nine pounds. Height – fifty-six pounds? Forearm measurement – *forearm* measurement?! Forty-seven inches? God, a mutant cud.... Anyway—

Flipping through the book.

... clove hitch, clove hitch.... Here we are. Mmmm.... Actually, that wasn't a clove hitch at all. It was a bowline. No wonder I failed cuds. Anyway, it looks as if all I really need is a simple slip knot...

He ties one, checking the book, humming "Bonanza" by Jay Livingston and Ray Evans.

Dum dede dum dede dum dede dum – Bonanza! – etc.

He gets the knot tied easily enough – holds it up – and we see that what he's made looks very much like a noose.

He continues humming "Bonanza," looks around for a place to string it up – stops.

What? Look, just keep whatever you're thinking to yourselves. The state has no business in the cud packs of the nation.

He throws the rope up over something. It falls.

Story of my life.

At this moment, something else in the box catches his eye. He takes it out, falls silent.

It's the torn half of an old photo.

(Note: Ideally the audience should see this photo projected on the scrim, or printed on the program. It shows a pretty girl of thirteen or so – vibrant, beaming, exuding joie de vivre. *The image has a sunny, summery feel to it.)*

He stares at it – ruminating, remembering.

Marisa...

A soft, shadowy light comes up behind the scrim, suggesting the flickering of a campfire. (We may hear a fragment of one of the campfire songs from the beginning.) TOBY turns to watch and it's as if, through the scrim, he's looking into his past.

We see a girl, MARISA, silhouetted, beckoning to someone.

MARISA Come on! My parents are here already! We don't have much time!

During this, the lights go down on TOBY. He steps off – and reappears behind the scrim with MARISA, in manner and body language magically thirteen years old again. (Note – these are not children. These are adult actors playing thirteen-year-olds.)

TOBY *(a bit shy and tongue-tied)* I… I wrote you this.

MARISA What is it?

TOBY Uh, sort of, a poem… I guess… here.

MARISA *(takes it, reads)* You are my sun,
You are my moon,
You are my shining star.
Locked in my heart is where you'll be—
'Til I am where you are…

You wrote this?

TOBY Don't you like it?

MARISA I love it.

TOBY Really?

MARISA It's beautiful.

TOBY This is for you too—

He gives her a photo.

It's… us.

She says nothing, close to tears.

What?

MARISA It's just… I feel like this is goodbye. Forever.

TOBY Why? We'll see each other next summer

MARISA We don't know that! My stupid parents are talking about moving to stupid Vancouver and…

A car horn honks.

WOMAN *(off)* Marisa! Time to go!

MARISA What if we're doomed to wander alone in the desert for the rest of our lives, parched and desperate, always missing each other, never knowing that the other was just beyond the next sand dune?!

TOBY But why would we be in a desert?

MARISA An emotional desert. It's a metaphor.

TOBY Oh.

MARISA It's unbearable!

She suddenly has an idea. She takes a barrette from her hair and jabs her finger.

TOBY What are you doing?!

She uses the barrette to write something on the back of the photo, in blood. Then she carefully tears the photo down the middle

Marisa?

MARISA *(gives him half)* Read it.

TOBY August 31, 2006. What's that?

MARISA That's exactly thirty-one years from today. I want us to make a solemn vow that we'll meet on that day.

TOBY But why thirty-one years?

MARISA We met August 1st. It's a year for each day we've known each other.

She gives him the barrette.

Stab your finger.

TOBY Me?! Why?!

WOMAN *(off)* Marisa!

MARISA Just do it. Please—

He jabs his finger with extreme reluctance, yelps.

TOBY God! I'm bleeding!

MARISA That's the point, silly. Take my hand—

She squeezes their two hands together.

—and swear by our blood which will mix and mingle in our veins forever that we'll meet on that day – and neither rain or sleet or typhoons or life's long and weary way will stop us. Or pestilence.

TOBY What's pestilence?

MARISA It's, it's – you know. Just swear, please?

TOBY Okay. I swear.

The car horn honks repeatedly.

MARISA I'm coming! *(throws her arms around TOBY and kisses him)* You are my sun… you are my moon…

She runs off tearfully, waving.

TOBY stands looking after her as the light fades to black behind the scrim…

… and TOBY re-enters in front of the scrim, an adult again, the torn photo in his hand.

TOBY *(half to himself)* … you are my shining star.
Locked in my heart is where you'll be
'Til I am where you are…
Marisa, Marisa…

He looks at the back of the photo.

August 31, 2006. God, that's tomorrow… thirty-one years.

He shakes himself out of his reverie.

Where does the time go when you're having fun fun fun?

He starts putting the photo and the other stuff back in the box – then stops.

What? Oh, come on. You don't expect me to actually *do* anything about this, do you? I mean, seriously, assuming I could even find her – what am I going to do? Call her up out of the blue? Turn up on her doorstep? Yoo hoo, it's me, my name is Pinky Lee! Hey, babe, it's been thirty-one years, but how about a cappucino? A San Pellegrino? A meaningful relationship? Does this reek of unreality or what? We were thirteen years old, for God's sake! What kind of emotionally arrested goof would even *remember* something like this?! *Buzzzz.* What is this kind, Alex. *(à la Alex Trebek)* Right you are, panelist. Select again—

Hopeless Romantic Fantasies for 400, please Alex.

(à la Alex Trebek) Hopeless indeed, panelist. For 400. The beautiful cousin you never get up your nerve to declare your love for, so you pour out your emotions in someone else's name…

He squeezes a broken buzzer.

Buzzzz. Who is – poor old Cyrano. Too easy, Alex.

For 600 – the love that keeps you going for thousands of miles through lashing storms and raging floods and attacks by mountain lions and possibly even pestilence!

Buzzzz.

What is – no, wait. That's *The Incredible Journey* – that's two dogs and a cat! Trick question, Alex, you sneaky devil.

Finally – ding, ding! For the Daily Double – the girl on the rope swing at camp. You're pushing her and she's swinging higher and higher, laughing, the sunlight glinting in her hair. And you're lightheaded, almost giddy because you've glimpsed life's unlimited possibilities. And you're haunted still by the idea that if somehow you'd grabbed onto that moment and never let it go, how different your life might have been… how different… and even now, you think – what if – what if you could somehow find her and recapture the clear blue innocence of that time – then you could recapture something in yourself… what is…

Silence.

Right. That's this story. Hey, I've even got a title – Loser Looks Up Love of His Life. Or how about – No Weddings and—

He holds up the noose.

—a Funeral? Or, it would be this story, except I'm not going to do anything about it. This one's a non-starter, no-hoper, no way José-er.

He gathers up the shoe box and heads off.

Finito.

He's all but off stage when he stops.

Oh, I know what you're thinking. You're thinking, I'm sitting here alone, *talking to Alex Trebek and imaginary people who apparently live in my wall!* You're thinking I'm at rope's end emotionally, financially, sartorially – so why in God's name don't I get off my Tubby Bum and do something?! So who asked you?

Again, he heads off… then abruptly turns back and walks to the desk.

Oh, all right. Just to shut you up…

He types on a laptop.

You think I can just Google her after thirty-one years and she'll actually appear—

Tapping and clicking.

—same name, no problem, on a platter, waiting for Prince Tubby. You really think life is that…

He stops abruptly, stares at the computer. It's obvious that her name has come up.

… simple.

Blackout.

Transitional music (perhaps "Countin' Flowers on the Wall", or the "Bonanza" theme).

Scene Two

Scrim rises, lights up to reveal MARISA's living room.

It's tastefully decorated with a bit of an artistic bent. The room has a lived-in, somewhat cluttered look, bordering on messy. Newspapers and takeout food containers clutter the coffee table. A large, half-full green garbage bag is sitting on the floor. There's a front door on one side. An open archway leads off to other parts of the house.

TOBY enters downstage. (There's a narrow, slightly lower playing area downstage, suggestive of a sidewalk outside the house.)

TOBY looks subtly spruced up, wearing a fresh shirt and jacket, hair combed. But he's the picture of tension, clutching a single rose wrapped in plastic.

He hesitates, stands on tiptoe, strains, jumps, as if trying to get a peek through the front window, but there's no one to be seen.

He approaches the front door, is puzzled, somewhat taken aback, to see a huge bouquet of flowers propped outside the door. It's far more lavish than his rather paltry offering, and he tries to get a look at the card attached to it, but it's sealed.

He raises his hand to ring the bell, once, twice, hesitates, loses his nerve.

TOBY Oh, come on! Am I a man or a cub?!

But he can't bring himself to ring.

I shouldn't just barge in. I should phone first.

He takes a cell phone from his pocket, but can't get up the nerve to dial. He paces back and forth, churning with indecision.

What's the worst that can happen? She'll laugh in my face. She'll call 9-1-1 and have me arrested as a stalker. I'll do ten years hard time surrounded by thieves and murderers and Conrad Black.... Or maybe, just maybe, she'll be won over by my bumbling charm and self-deprecating wit, and encyclopedic knowledge of useless trivia – and taste in flowers...

He has a thought, glances around – quickly goes and takes the large bouquet, pulls the card off, switches them, leaving the single rose with the card by the door instead.

Desperate times, desperate measures. And she'll fall into my arms and say – what are you doing for the rest of your life, big boy?... Don't scoff. It's possible.

He abruptly punches buttons on the cell phone.

Into the Valley of Death rode the Prince Tubby...

He waits, holding his breath. A phone rings in the living room.

She's probably not there. I'll get a machine.

MARISA appears in the archway.

She's forty-five-ish now, still very attractive. And she's wearing what looks suspiciously like a wedding dress. It's unzipped in back as if she's just been trying it on. She's struggling to reach back and zip it up as she hears the phone.

Just say something simple but witty. You're Bogey.
No, Cary Grant…

MARISA hurries across the room to get it as the answering machine clicks in—

MARISA *(on machine)* Hi, this is Marisa. Leave a message.

TOBY Hello, kiddo. This is a voice out of the mists and pestilence of time—

MARISA *(grabs the phone during this)* Hello! Merry Maids?

TOBY jumps, drops the phone like a hot potato, discombobulated by the sound of her real voice.

Molly Maids?… Maids of any sort?

TOBY stares at the phone on the ground, frozen.

Hello?… Hello?!…

TOBY *(hissing at himself)* Speak now or forever be a hopeless loser!

MARISA What?!

TOBY Speak!

MARISA Hello?!…

TOBY *(at the phone on the ground)* Hello.

MARISA I can't hear you! Is this Merry Maids?

TOBY picks up the phone, gets blasted by her shout.

Hello?!

TOBY Uh – Marisa?

MARISA Yes! Who is this?

TOBY What is pestilence exactly?

MARISA What?

TOBY Nothing. Just an icebreaker, a conversational gambit. You forgot your appointment.

MARISA What?! Who? Where? What have I forgotten now?

TOBY It's August 31, 2006.

MARISA It's tomorrow.

TOBY *(surprised)* So you did remember?

MARISA Of course I remembered.

TOBY But it's today.

MARISA Oh, no! Don't tell me the date was wrong on the invitations.

TOBY Invitations? Are you having a party?

MARISA A party? Isn't this about the wedding?

TOBY Wedding? Whose wedding?

MARISA My wedding!

TOBY *(stunned)* You're getting married?! Today?!

MARISA Tomorrow, not today.

TOBY You're getting married tomorrow?

MARISA Yes! Who *is* this?!

TOBY *(pause)* Is this a firm decision?

MARISA Who is this?

TOBY *(covers the phone)* I wait thirty-one years – *thirty-one years!* – and end up calling her the day before her wedding day! Typical, typical, *typical…*

MARISA What?! I can't hear you!

TOBY "As flies to wanton boys are we to the gods. They pull off our wings and stab pins through our hearts and kill us for their sport."

MARISA *King Lear?*

TOBY God! Not only beautiful, but literate! It's too much to bear!

MARISA Who is this, for heaven's sake?!

TOBY No one. No one at all.

He hangs up.

MARISA Damn!

He stands there and gives an unintelligible yowl of frustration at the heavens.

MARISA looks at the messy room in despair, picks up the garbage bag, goes to the door. She has a thought and picks up the mobile phone.

(presses buttons on the phone) Star sixty-nine…

TOBY walks away, tosses the flowers on the ground.

MARISA comes out the door on the side opposite to him, downstage, carrying the garbage bag to the curb.

He glances back and sees her, freezes.

For a few moments the scene now becomes stylized. The light softens. We hear a few bars of obvious romantic music.

TOBY stands there, staring, mesmerized at the sight of MARISA after thirty-one years. She walks towards him in dreamy slow motion, in her wedding dress, like a parody of hokey reunion scenes seen in countless movies.

He opens his arms as if for the big Hollywood embrace.

She presses a button on her mobile phone.

His cell (now in his pocket) rings jarringly as she plops down the garbage bag unceremoniously, breaking the fantasy.

His cell rings again. He slaps at his pocket, trying to shut it off. But MARISA scarcely notices him, doesn't seem to connect the call she's making with the ringing in this stranger's pocket.

He turns away, trying to make himself inconspicuous, manages to silence the pocketed phone after another ring or two.

Damn…

She heads back towards the house, paying scant attention to him.

TOBY stares after her. She pauses at the door, picks up the flower. Just before she goes back in, he grabs the large bouquet from the ground.

TOBY Aaaaaaah—

MARISA Yes? *(She stops by the door.)* Flowers?

TOBY Mmm?… I mean, yes, yes, flowers – precisely – Rosebud Florists. Flowers for all your… floral needs.

He crosses and thrusts them at her.

MARISA Rosebud. Very "Citizen Kane." Thank you.

She turns to go in. He just stands there.

TOBY Um—

MARISA Yes.

TOBY You're welcome.

He makes no move to go.

MARISA Sorry. I don't have any change.

TOBY Oh, I have change.

Fishing out a handful.

How much do you need?

MARISA I meant for you.

TOBY For me? Oh. No no. No no no. No no no.

She turns again to go in.

What did you think of it? "Citizen Kane"?

MARISA Well, that's sort of like asking what I think of the Sistine Chapel. They don't make 'em like that any more.

TOBY No kidding. Films today. Talk about a load of pestilent excrement that beggars the powers of human description.

MARISA Mmhm – well, I'd better get these in water.

TOBY And be sure and put in that little packet of chemical sprinkly stuff it keeps them alive longer. Not that they're alive, they're dead, but they don't know that and it fools them into thinking there's still, you know – hope.

She's not quite sure what to say to this and again turns to go.

It's like Orson Welles he was twenty-five when he made "Kane" and the world was his oyster and he had no way of knowing then that the rest of his life would be an inexorable slide into frustration failure despair obesity and—

MARISA Wine commercials.

TOBY Exactly exactly exactly. It's Toby. Boone.

She looks at him blankly.

Toby Boone.

MARISA *(no flicker of recognition)* Yes?

TOBY We were at Camp Kippewa together.

MARISA We were? Well, you must have quite a memory.

TOBY The curse of an under-utilized mind. The things I remember. Don't get me started.

MARISA I think you've already started.

TOBY A pile of useless crap most of it. Not you! I don't mean you. It's certainly worth remembering, uh, you – I'm not making you uneasy am I?!

MARISA *(uneasily)* Not at all. So, now you're the Rosebud Florist man?

TOBY Countin' flowers on the wall, that don't bother me at all… actually, no, I'm, I'm Director General of Cub Scouts International. Spelled with a "b" by the way.

MARISA Really. How… interesting.

TOBY Actually, I'm not. That was a joke.

MARISA A cub joke?

TOBY Yeah, it's a highly specialized field. Cub humour. If you ever need a clovehitch, or a killer cub joke *(à la Leonard Cohen)* I'm your man…. *(She just looks at him.)* God this is going badly! Are you sure I'm not making you uneasy?!

MARISA Did you just phone here? A few minutes ago?

TOBY Me? No, no – no – no – *(She just looks at him.)* Well, sort of…

MARISA Hey, you can't be half pregnant. You can't be half phoned.

TOBY *(bursts out laughing, too loudly – abruptly stops himself)* Sorry, I – I don't do good phone. I'm not handy with these newfangled concepts – phones, talking pictures, interpersonal relationships— Anyway, I just wanted to see you – I always thought I'd see you – once – again –

He stops.

MARISA Well, nice to see you again too – uh—

TOBY Toby.

MARISA Toby?

Trying to remember.

Camp Kippewa? So you're not really the Rosebud Florist man?

He shakes his head.

So these flowers are from—?

TOBY Me.

MARISA Sorry, but I don't understand. I mean, they're very nice, albeit dead. But if you didn't know I was getting married, or even if you did, why would you?

TOBY Turn up on your doorstep after thirty-one years bearing flowers?

MARISA And cracking cub jokes?

TOBY Listen, this whole thing is sort of like… a crop circle. It defies rational explanation. Little aliens came down at night and trampled my brain until it was all flat and weird and made me do foolish things.

MARISA Fascinating. Well, I've got fifty people coming for a reception tomorrow and Merry Maids has abandoned me. So thanks for the flowers and an… unusual conversation.

TOBY Unusual? Oh, I have conversations like this all the time. With myself…. That was a joke. Actually, it's not a joke. It's true…. *God this is going badly!* Look, I'm off. In more ways than one you may be thinking. I'll let you get ready for your bar mitzvah, or whatever.

MARISA My wedding.

TOBY Right. I knew it was a function of some sort. Well, bye. And hey, we'll always have Camp Kippewa.

MARISA "Casablanca"?

TOBY Yeah, too easy. The 200-dollar question.

MARISA Unusual.

She goes back inside, closes the door.

TOBY doesn't budge. He kind of slumps over, leans his head against the door, moaning softly.

(to herself) Toby Boone… Toby Boone…

She suddenly has a thought, goes back and opens the door.

TOBY's still standing there, his head leaning against the door, so he half falls into the room when she opens it. She jumps—

TOBY Sorry. I was just—

MARISA Leaning your head on my door. Toby Boone. Are you Tobias Boone? The film critic?

TOBY I am – I was.

MARISA Why didn't you say so?

TOBY Well, it's never been much of a chick magnet.

MARISA You do better with that Cub Scout International line?

TOBY Oh, every time. That cub stuff, it slays them.

MARISA Well, consider me slain. Come in for a minute.

He comes in, looks around.

So, Tobias Boone. I used to be quite a film nut. Not an expert like you, of course. Just small potatoes.

TOBY Oh, don't apologize – for your potatoes.

MARISA I was on the board of the film society here. We used your quotes in our program a couple of times. Not that often because, well, we were trying to promote the films and you—

TOBY Generally panned them. I know. It's my one semi-marketable skill – vivisecting pretentious crap with savage surgical precision and leaving it in bleeding chunks on the floor! *(a beat)* So, seen anything good lately?

MARISA Uh, no.… You?

TOBY Silly question.

They stand there, out of small talk already. A beat of awkward silence.

MARISA I used to read your reviews in the *Star*. But I don't think I've seen your name lately?

TOBY Yeah, they eliminated me a while back. The last straw was when I panned "Sideways."

MARISA Oh, I loved that.

TOBY Well, you're wrong.

MARISA It's how I felt. How you feel can't be wrong, can it? The reasons of the heart are never wrong. Someone said something like that. Aristotle – or was it Oprah?

TOBY Anyway, "Sideways" was totally ludicrous! Here's this nerd, this whiner, this ugly little *loser* who has this absolute babe getting all hot for him. Why?! Because he knows about *wine!* Because he knows a Pinot Noir from a friggin' Merlot! – and there's nothing wrong with a nice Merlot, by the way. And I have the nerve to point out that this is nothing but a Hollywood fantasy of the most juvenile kind, that this would never, ever happen in the real world, ever – that a woman like that would fall for a nebbish like him because he knows about wine, or films, or—

MARISA She didn't fall for him because of wine. She sensed a deeper connection, that there was something under—

TOBY His ugly exterior.

MARISA He wasn't ugly. And women don't care about that sort of thing—

TOBY Such a lie.

MARISA —as much as men.

TOBY Anyway, I'm between engagements right now, as we say in the biz. So I'm actually trying to write a book at the moment.

MARISA *(interested)* Oh?

TOBY Yeah, it's called *Crap, Crap and More Crap – My Life As a Critic.* I'm thinking of dropping the last three words.

MARISA Well, I'm sure you'll find something if you get out there and look.

TOBY Oh, I found exactly what I was looking for but it burped and fizzled and came to nothing.

MARISA Why?

TOBY She's getting married in the morning.

Silence. She looks a bit uncomfortable.

MARISA The afternoon.... How did you find me?

TOBY Oh, I had millions of little buggers out beating the bushes. And they always get their man, those Royal Canadian Mounted Cubs.

MARISA *(laughs)* Sorry, I don't know why I don't remember you. You're quite—

TOBY Memorable?

MARISA Different. But it was a long time ago.

TOBY Oh, I was different then, too. I sometimes feel as if I've been different since the womb. I bet when the doctor pulled me out he held me up and said, "It's a boy! It's... different."

She sort of laughs, not sure how to take him.

MARISA Anyway, I was only at camp one summer for—

TOBY Thirty-one days. And then your stupid parents moved to stupid Vancouver.

MARISA Boy, you remember a lot. I just remember the odd incident. There was one time, with that rope swing—

TOBY I pushed you on that rope swing once.

MARISA You did?

TOBY You kept squealing – higher! Higher!

MARISA Mmm. Get a glimpse of anything you shouldn't have?

TOBY Life's unlimited possibilities.

MARISA ... I don't remember that, but I remember one day some of the boys took the rope and tied it to a tree at the top of that hill up the shoreline from the camp – more of a cliff really. And they'd run and swing out over the edge and drop into the water, whooping like hormone-crazed Tarzans, showing off for the girls.

TOBY Mmhm.

MARISA You remember?

TOBY Mmhm.

MARISA And there was this one boy – he was kind of fat and unathletic and he was obviously scared stiff. But the other boys kept goading him, calling him a sissy, shaming him into it. Some of the girls, too—

TOBY Mmhm.

MARISA He ran towards the cliff and started his swing, but the knot let go—

TOBY Probably a clove hitch.

MARISA —and he fell and – oh, God I can still see this – he bounced! And he kept bouncing and rolling and bouncing and rolling all the way down. And everyone was laughing hysterically until he reached the bottom. He just lay there, face down in the water, not moving. And suddenly everything went deathly still. It was Brett, Brett Bradley, who ran down and pulled him out.

TOBY Golden Boy.

MARISA He was all right, just banged up. But he could have been killed. I don't remember his name. They had a nickname for him – Fatso or Lard Ass or—

TOBY Tubby Bum.

MARISA Tubby Bum! That was it. I wonder what became of him—

He just looks at her. A long beat.

MARISA No… no…

TOBY Toby Boone – Tubby Bum.

MARISA I'm so sorry! I feel like a fool!

TOBY No problem. It's nice to be remembered.

MARISA But you're not exactly tubby now, you're…

TOBY Size-Appropriate-for-a-Middle-Aged-Critic Bum now, I guess. But, he's still inside here somewhere, screaming to get out. Once a Tubby Bum, always a Tubby Bum – *(points to his head)* – in here.

MARISA I don't believe that. People can grow.

TOBY Nah.

MARISA People can change.

TOBY Nah.

MARISA For better or worse.

TOBY To coin a phrase.

MARISA Which reminds me, sorry, I've got a thousand things to do before—

TOBY The solemn nuptials.

MARISA Oh. Would you mind zipping me up?

TOBY Oh. Yes. I mean no –

She turns her half-bare back to him. He fumbles nervously with the zipper, all thumbs—

Sorry. I don't zip much.

—but he gets it done up.

MARISA Thanks. Does this dress look all right?

TOBY No – it looks perfect.

Another slightly awkward beat.

MARISA Well, it was nice to meet you, to see you again – Toby.

This is his signal to go. He starts for the door – abruptly turns back.

TOBY So that's your Camp Kippewa memory? You don't remember anything else about, well, the last day?

MARISA I do actually, but it was private—

TOBY shrugs – if you say so.

You mean the vow? But that was with Brett. Did he tell you about that?

TOBY Golden Boy? Are you kidding? He forgot it five minutes after he made it. But I remembered it… and there's this.

He produces the torn half of the photo. She looks at it in amazement – the date written in blood on the back.

MARISA August 31, 2006.

TOBY Today.

MARISA I've still got the other half of this somewhere.

TOBY In a shoe box probably, with the skull of your dead hamster and your little Girl Guides cap.

MARISA Brownie cap. But where did you get this? Did you steal it?

TOBY I – rescued it.

MARISA You stole it.

TOBY Okay, I stole it from the floor of Golden Boy's locker. That's where it was, under some stinking socks and rotting jockstraps and used—

MARISA All right, all right.

TOBY And he never missed it! We weren't back at school for a week before he'd taken up with some cheerleader. Judy Gluck to be precise. I doubt you ever crossed his mind again.

MARISA You don't know that.

TOBY Ah, you knew him for a month – in the hormonal hothouse of a coed summer camp. I spent five years in high school with him. He's the one who stuck me with that nickname. And, of course, he'd saved my friggin' life, sort of, which gave me another reason to despise him. He was a smug, egocentric—

MARISA He was a bit self-absorbed—

TOBY —jerk.

MARISA But there was a sensitive side to Brett. He wrote me the sweetest poem.

TOBY Really.

MARISA I still have it.

TOBY Let me guess. Did it go something like this?

"You are my sun
You are my moon
You are my shining star—
Locked in my heart
Is where you'll be
'Til I am where you are."

MARISA How do you…? Were you spying on us?!

TOBY *(shrugs)* That's not why I know the poem.... I know it because I wrote it.

MARISA You didn't.

TOBY You really think he could have written that? Golden No Brain?

MARISA But... why would you write a poem for *him*?

TOBY He asked me. He said you were a sucker for that sort of thing.

MARISA Why didn't you give it to me yourself?

TOBY I was Tubby Bum. You were Golden Girl. You wouldn't have paid any attention to a poem from me.

MARISA I might have.

TOBY Not in a million years. I could never touch you, obviously, but this way I could touch you with my words without you even knowing it. And I did. I heard the catch in your voice as you read my poem—

MARISA Sneaky little spying person.

TOBY Saw the tears running down your cheeks as you drove off gazing out the window of your parents' car. And that image has stayed with me for thirty-one years.

MARISA Thirty-one years! We were children!

TOBY Arrested development, *c'est moi.*

MARISA But none of this makes sense.

TOBY It does to me. I've always lived a sort of vicarious life. Even as an adult, so-called, sitting alone in dark theatres, watching make-believe, and then writing about it as if it were real, as if it mattered, while real life was going on outside on the streets, in the sunshine and the garbage – just out of reach. And I replayed that goodbye scene in my mind so many times, over and over, that I started imagining it was my hand you were stabbing with that pin, my eyes you were gazing into.

MARISA Come on.

TOBY Those were my words that caused those tears, that prompted you to make that vow. He was there physically, but I was there in spirit—

MARISA And in the bushes. But why turn up now? You knew perfectly well I'd made that vow with Brett, not you.

TOBY But I knew he wouldn't keep it.

MARISA So were you going to pretend to be him?

TOBY Of course not! That would be ridiculous and probably immoral.

MARISA And doomed to failure. So why are you here?

TOBY Well, I guess I thought, I hoped, that if I showed up and finally told you the truth that you'd – I don't know – respond somehow. If I spread my dreams beneath your feet that you'd tread softly.

MARISA You are a poet.

TOBY No, but Yeats is. Look. I don't know what I thought. The whole thing is nonsensical, pathetic, childish – supply your own adjective.

MARISA *(a beat)* Romantic?… The reasons of the heart are never wrong, as whatsisname said.

Silence. Neither knows quite what to say.

Well, I guess that explains why he didn't remember the poem very well. Even when I showed it to him.

TOBY Showed it—?

MARISA You see, you're wrong about a few things. He did remember the vow – Brett. He called me on August 31.

TOBY *This* is August 31.

MARISA Three years ago.

TOBY Three years ago?! But that's twenty-eight years! It was a thirty-one-year vow! Thirty-one years for thirty-one days! How can you confuse twenty-eight with thirty-one?! Did he think we were at camp in February?!

MARISA Well, he was only three years off—

TOBY What a moron!

MARISA —and you'd stolen the picture with the date on it.

TOBY Rescued. So what did he say? What did he want?

MARISA *(shrugs)* What does anyone want?

TOBY I can imagine. I hope you told him to get lost.

MARISA Well, to tell you the truth—

TOBY I hate the truth. Give me fiction any day.

MARISA My marriage had broken up—

TOBY You were married?

MARISA —and I was feeling a bit bruised emotionally, and lo and behold, my first big crush turns up out of the blue. And call me shallow, but he was still one good-looking guy.

TOBY You said women don't care about that!

MARISA Well—

TOBY You lied.

MARISA I lied. On our first date we went cycling—

TOBY You *dated* him?!

MARISA —and he turned up in one of those form-fitting-leave nothing-to-the-imagination Lance Armstrong jobs.

TOBY He won you over with Spandex?!

MARISA You know what they say – his suit was so tight I couldn't breathe.

TOBY How long did you "date" him for?

MARISA A while.

TOBY Well? Weeks? Months?… Years?

She doesn't answer.

When did it end?…

The penny drops.

It didn't end? You don't mean – he's not – you're not marrying HIM?!

No answer is necessary.

"As flies to wanton boys…"

To the heavens.

What more can you do to me?!… Don't answer that.

He turns to go.

Well, it's your funeral.

MARISA Wedding.

TOBY Same difference. Music, mumbo jumbo and eternal hell and damnation.

MARISA I guess I'll take that as congratulations.

TOBY Where is he, anyway?

MARISA Playing golf. He should be back any minute if you'd like to say hello…

He just gives her a look.

Or not.

TOBY So he never told you? The truth about the poem?

MARISA No, but who cares what happened when we were thirteen? We moved on from that pretty quickly.

TOBY Moved on. Yeah. That's something I never quite mastered. I should see if there's a book on that – *Moving On For Dummies.*

He pauses by the door.

Sorry I didn't bring you a present.

MARISA You brought me flowers.

TOBY Deluded dead ones. Don't forget the little sprinkly stuff. Fool them into thinking that life is worth living.

MARISA I'm sorry.

TOBY No, no, no. The universe is unfolding as it always does. Golden Boy gets the girl, Tubby Bum gets the gears. The fundamental things apply as time goes by.

MARISA Maybe you let too much time go by. Who knows what might have happened if you'd tried this sooner.

TOBY It wouldn't have made the slightest difference.

He opens the door to go.

I'm searching for an appropriate send-off – Pithy Exit Lines for 200, Alex…. "Frankly my dear I don't give a damn"… Nah. "This is the beginning of a beautiful friendship."… Hardly. How about "*Hasta la vista*, baby." But then I'm supposed to shoot you.

MARISA Maybe you should stop trying to think of a line from the movies, and come up with one of your own. From the heart. Try connecting with real people, real life, a little more.

TOBY I did. Today. I grabbed onto that rope and swung out over the abyss and went bouncing down the hill all over again. And you two are still standing at the top, laughing your heads off.

He heads out.

MARISA Damn you, I'm not laughing! And you're not going anywhere.

TOBY I'm not?

MARISA *(grabs him, pulls him back in)* Not until you promise to cut out all this self-pity crap. And I don't want to hear any more references to movies, or to Tubby Bum, or bouncing down that hill, or any other stupid thing that happened thirty years ago that any normal person would have forgotten twenty-nine years ago – or to cubs!

He's silent.

Well?

TOBY Nothing. I'm reference-less. I'm up the creek without my schtick.

MARISA *(almost laughs)* I mean it's easy for you.

TOBY What?

MARISA This.

TOBY This?! This is the hardest thing I've ever done in my life! Well, since sitting through "Deuce Bigelow, European Gigolo" anyway.

MARISA Oh, come on. You just drop in out of the blue sky, all bumbling charm and obscure little jokes and—

TOBY You find me charming – in a bumbling, jokey sort of way?

MARISA See. It's all about you. Have you asked a single question about me? About my life? Charmed or otherwise?

TOBY Well – I—

MARISA Go ahead. Ask me a question.

TOBY Are you happy?

MARISA *(snaps)* Of course. Isn't it obvious? Anyway, happiness is overrated.

TOBY I wouldn't know. Never tried it.

MARISA Next question.

TOBY What do you do? You and Golden Spandex Boy?

MARISA Well, we golf. We—

TOBY Golf!

MARISA Well, *he* golfs. I think the happiest I've ever seen him was when he got something called a Big Bertha. He bought me a new set of Little Berthas, or whatever. But I couldn't hit the little piece of shit worth shit.

TOBY It's called a ball.

MARISA But we're mature adults. We pursue our own interests. We don't have to do everything together like wussy dependent people.

TOBY In other words, you have nothing whatsoever in common?

She says nothing.

What does he do for a living?

MARISA *(hesitates)* He has – he has two Red Lobsters.

A beat, then TOBY bursts out laughing.

What?! What's so funny?!

She starts laughing as well, in spite of herself.

He owns two Red Lobster franchises.

TOBY Have another calamari, Golden Boy! It's just so – just so – perfect.

MARISA He's very successful. You're just jealous.

TOBY Not at all. I'm successful too. Look at it this way – if the definition of a critic is a failed human being, and I'm a failed critic, that makes me a failed failure – ergo – a success. So, what else do you and Lobster Boy do? Other than fighting over the jumbo shrimp in the giant seafood platter?

MARISA We have mad, passionate sex constantly.

TOBY Now you're just trying to hurt me.

MARISA And we travel.

TOBY Where? To Red Lobster conventions?

We can tell from her reaction that he's hit close to home.

MARISA And other places.

TOBY His condo in Florida?

MARISA *(He's hit close to home again.)* Arizona, actually. It's very nice. And other places. Italy.

TOBY Italy? I always wanted to go to Italy. So, how was it?

MARISA It was fabulous.

He looks at her.

It was nice.

Silence.

It was okay. Look, it had been my dream trip for years. Sometimes it's hard for reality to measure up to a dream.

TOBY Yeah.

MARISA Anyway, give the guy credit. He agreed to go as long as he had a week in Scotland first playing golf, so I went on ahead to Florence. And I wandered around the museums and churches and sat in the Piazzas and sipped my Orvieto Classico and listened to street musicians in a kind of golden haze of delight. I just felt as if – as if I'd come home.

TOBY But…?

MARISA No buts.

TOBY But.

MARISA Well, Brett arrived. And it sounds petty, but just the little things he'd do would bug me. He'd order pizza and say it wasn't as good as Domino's. He'd call the waiters *senor* and *senorita* – and on top of it all he was positively squirming with boredom from the moment he got there. We lined up for an hour to see the David, and I just knew he was thinking – why am I staring at some big, naked guy with a slingshot when I could be on a golf course somewhere?

TOBY With Big Bertha.

MARISA I don't even know why I'm telling you this.

TOBY The heart has its reasons.

MARISA Anyway, one day we were on that bridge – the Ponte Vecchio – and suddenly, walking by, no one paying the slightest attention, was Helena Bonham Carter. It was like an epiphany. "Room With a View" is my all time fave Italian film—

TOBY Well, you're wrong there. Dare I mention "8 1/2"?

MARISA Stop it, film boy.

TOBY "The Bicycle Thief."

MARISA *(ignores him)* There she was. Six feet away from us.

TOBY "L'Avventura."

MARISA I whispered to Brett. Look, it's Helena Bonham Carter!

TOBY Did he have a clue—?

MARISA Who she was? Not the faintest. And then a ridiculous thing happened. She was wearing just what you'd expect Helena Bonham Carter to wear—

TOBY Mmm, some sort of long summer dress –

MARISA A long, billowing, flowered dress. Very good.

TOBY I know my obscure movie star couture.

MARISA And suddenly a gust of wind caught her dress and blew it up – just like that Marilyn Monroe scene – and for a second we got, well, a pretty spectacular view of—

TOBY Life's unlimited possibilities?

MARISA More like Helena's unlimited bum. I think she was wearing a thong.

TOBY Helena Bonham Carter?! A *thong?!* Are you sure it wasn't Pamela Anderson?

MARISA She just laughed and shoved her skirt down and kept walking. Of course, this was the first thing on the whole trip that got Brett's undivided attention. And he said, "are you sure her name isn't Helena Bum Bum Carter?"

TOBY What a wit. Clear a spot at the Algonquin Round Table.

MARISA It was funny at the time. And it was one of those quirky, perfect little Italy moments, like something out of a Fellini movie—

TOBY Possibly "8 1/2".

MARISA Except from then on everywhere we went – every restaurant, every shop – he'd say ooh, do you think we'll see Bum Bum Carter? Ooh, isn't that Bum Bum Carter. It was driving me crazy. Anyway, one afternoon we were in the Botticelli Room at the Uffizi – and I could hear him catch his breath, and he grabbed my arm, and I thought, silly me, that finally the power of all this art is getting to him – and he said – Look! It's Bum Bum! And I just lost it. I started screaming at him – Stop it! *Stop it!* You're ruining my trip! You're ruining my life! Of course I didn't mean it – that he was ruining my life.
My life isn't ruined at all. It's very… comfortable.

TOBY Comfortable.

MARISA Look, just because he prefers Big Bertha to Botticelli doesn't make him a bad person. And he was all apologetic and a complete sweetheart for the rest of the trip. On the flight home, he got us upgraded to first class—

TOBY There's gold in them there lobsters.

MARISA And after about the third free drink he proposed. We also agreed that we should probably take separate vacations.

TOBY Don't do it.

MARISA I think separate vacations are a perfectly good—

TOBY Don't marry him.

MARISA It will be all right.

TOBY All right?! *All right?!* You're going to settle for all right when you could have…

MARISA When I could have what?

TOBY Me?

MARISA You? What have you got to offer?

TOBY *(pause)* Give me a minute.

MARISA He'll be back in a minute. You have thirty seconds. What is it you're offering? Precisely?

TOBY Oh, God.... Well, there's – there's a love that's kept going for thirty-one years and – and will keep going for thirty-one more, mile after mile through lashing storms and raging floods, and attacks by mountain lions and—

MARISA *(thinking)* Hold on a sec—

TOBY —and possibly even pestilence!

MARISA Isn't that some dog movie?

TOBY Nah.

MARISA It is. You're offering me thirty-one years of dog-like devotion?

TOBY And the bumbling charm. Come with me!

MARISA Come?! Where?

TOBY Anywhere. Around the block. Italy. We'll sit in the Piazza della Whatever and watch for Helena – and I'll know who she is – and it won't matter whether she walks by or not, because we'll – we'll be together.

MARISA It's crazy.

TOBY That's the point! Once every thirty-one years you have to do something crazy. And this is that moment! It's—

MARISA Please don't say it's the first day of the rest of our lives.

TOBY God! I'd never say that! Don't you know me at all after thirty-one years?! I hate those bumper sticker clichés!

MARISA Good.

TOBY So throw something in a bag! Now! *(she doesn't move)* It's the first day of the rest of our lives!

MARISA I can't just walk out without even speaking to him.

TOBY You have to! If you wait, he'll stroll in in his Spandex and sweet-talk you out of it.

MARISA You don't golf in Spandex.

TOBY If he walks in that door, the moment will be lost. You'll be doomed to be, to be – comfortable for the rest of your life. Because you're weak, you're shallow, you're fickle...

MARISA You're nuts.

TOBY *(takes her hands)*
… you're wonderful…
You were my sun
You were my moon
You were my shining star…
And still, my love, you are. You are. You are.

MARISA *(touched, a bit choked up)* It doesn't scan.

TOBY I'll work on it. I'll make it better. We'll make everything better. Together.

A car door slams.

MARISA It's him!

In a panic, she rushes to look out a window.

It's not him! It's just the nosy neighbour!

TOBY A standard device in cheap fiction.

MARISA Oh, God! I don't know what to do!

TOBY Then let me decide for you. Go! Pack!

MARISA *(starts out, hesitates)* But – I know you're charming, and witty, and different, and possibly even—

TOBY Yes?

MARISA —lovable – but even you admitted, you're sort of – useless.

TOBY I've changed. That was the old me, the me of twenty minutes ago. Now I feel a wave of usefulness flowing through me. I've banished my inner Tubby Bum! I'm not the schleppy secondary character any more! I'm the romantic lead! I'm – Alex Trebek! I've got all the answers. I'll take care of everything…. I'll take care of you.

She comes towards him.

What are you doing?

MARISA Promise?

She puts her arms around him, kisses him.

TOBY *(breathless)* I promise.

She turns her back to him, holds her hair up. He nuzzles her neck. She sighs. He moans softly.

Jan Alexandra Smith and Murray Furrow
photo by Dan Pritchard

MARISA Stop that! Unzip me! I have to change!

He unzips her dress, no fumbling this time, and she hurries to the archway, pauses, with playful suggestiveness.

I'll be back.

She exits. TOBY stands there, slightly dazed, then picks up paper and pen from a side table, starts to write, composing aloud.

TOBY Dear Not-So-Golden Boy – Eat your golden heart out, old buddy, old loser – no.

He scratches it out.

Be magnanimous. Be gracious in victory…

Dear Brett,

This is a voice out of the mists and pestilence of long ago. Marisa has chosen to follow the reasons of her heart – bracket, Aristotle, bracket – and spend the rest of her time on the rope swing of life with me. But look on the bright side, you still have Big Bertha.

MARISA comes back in with a suitcase. She's changed into a travelling outfit. He looks incredulous that she was so fast.

MARISA I was packed for the honeymoon.

TOBY *(quickly finishing the note)* Keep swinging – Tubby Bum – no—

He scratches it out.

The Artist Formerly Known as Tubby Bum.

MARISA *(laughing)* You're so clever.

She puts her arms around him.

You're so cute. What are you doing for the rest of your life, big boy?

We hear a car door slam.

TOBY That's our cue.

He leaves the note, grabs her hand, grabs the bag. Laughing like teenagers, they hurry out the front door.

MARISA Is this really happening?

They exit.

A beat. We hear a door open in the back of the house.

MAN'S VOICE *(off)* Marisa?! Honey? Guess what!… I had a hole in one!

Blackout (or possibly a more stylized light shift).

Lights up.

The garbage bag is again sitting in the middle of the room where it was before. The plastic-wrapped rose is again lying outside the front door.

TOBY is sitting alone on the curb with the big bouquet, staring into space in a kind of reverie, smiling faintly to himself.

TOBY "I had a hole in one. I had a hole in one." While Brett marches through the house, vaingloriously trumpeting his achievement to a succession of empty rooms, Toby and Marisa hail a cab and go straight to the airport, where they nab the last two seats, first class, on the overnight flight to Rome. They sip – Campari – and watch the movie – uh—

He thinks.

—"Roman Holiday" with Audrey Hepburn and Gregory Peck, and then fall asleep, cradled in each other's arms. At dawn, exhausted but thrillingly alive, they walk hand in hand through the rain-washed streets of the Eternal City and come upon the deserted Trevi Fountain where they splash and – cavort, yes, cavort, that's good, just like Marcello Mastroianni and Anita Ekberg in "La Dolce Vita." Then they dash off, giggling like teenagers, and head for that bridge – the famous one – the Ponte Vecchio! That's it – no wait, that's in Florence. They're in Rome. So where the hell do they go? Shit!

This suddenly snaps him out of his reverie. (It should be clear by now that he's imagined this whole preceding scenario.)

God! What am I doing?!

He stands, shaking himself back to reality.

Stop it! What's wrong with me?!

He looks at his watch.

God, an hour's gone by! Hey, just a few thousand more and my life will be over with. Always nice to have a little something to look forward to. Enough of this cheap fiction! In the name of all that's holy, in the name of Steve McQueen, just do it! Go to the door—

He does.

—ring the bell—

He raises his hand – can't do it. He tries to peer in the peephole.

Why do I feel like I'm still thirteen?!

He steps back, tries to see in the window again. He jumps two or three times, craning to see.

A WOMAN enters from the side, carrying a grocery bag. She stops short when she sees him. (We can't get a good look at her in slightly shadowy light, but it appears to be MARISA.)

TOBY hasn't noticed her. He reaches up as if grabbing the window ledge. Grunting with effort, he pulls himself up, trying to see in.

WOMAN Hey! What are you doing?!

TOBY yelps, loses his grip, falls to the ground, banging his chin, scraping his hand.

TOBY I'm not – it's not what it—

He scrambles to his feet. She grabs a can out of her bag, points it at him.

WOMAN Stay back! I've got Mace!

TOBY *(backing up)* No, no—

He looks at it.

That's not Mace. That's Easy-Off Oven Cleaner.

WOMAN Yeah, but have you seen what it does to human flesh?

TOBY No. I've never used it. I prefer to leave my oven with its natural protective coating. Of grease – Marisa?

WOMAN It's Zoe.

As she takes a step forward, into more light, we see that indeed it's not MARISA – but very much a younger version of her, perhaps twenty-four or twenty-five (and the same actress).

TOBY Who?

ZOE Her daughter.

TOBY Her daughter.... Well, look, I know this must look a bit, well, odd.

He picks up the flowers.

ZOE Not to mention creepy and illegal.

TOBY *(à la John Wayne)* But you can holster the oven cleaner, pilgrim.

ZOE Uh?

TOBY Sorry. When I'm nervous I lapse into stupid lines from stupid movies. That was John Wayne. Obviously.

She just looks at him dubiously.

Or not so obviously. The point is I'm completely harmless. You can't imagine how harmless I am. Harmless, thy name is me.

ZOE You're different than the others.

TOBY Different. You're very perceptive. What others?

ZOE The other men in her life, over the years.

TOBY Oh, I'm not a man in her life... at all. I'm just.... Anyway, sorry if the Peeping Tom routine startled you.

ZOE Oh, I think I understand. You wanted to check out the situation, before you barged in.

TOBY *(slightly puzzled)* Something like that, I guess. Her daughter! God, you could be—

ZOE Sisters. I know.

TOBY Does she have other children? A big family?

ZOE Just me. And don't believe a word you've heard. I'm a lot nicer now.

TOBY Oh, I haven't heard anything. So, are there other family members? Uncles? Cousins? A husband?

ZOE A husband? Not lately. You are out of touch. When did you last see Mum?

TOBY Oh, it's been, it's been… a while.

ZOE So how did you know?

TOBY Know?

ZOE About Mum.

TOBY Well, I knew her, sort of, years ago.

ZOE At university?

TOBY At camp.

ZOE At *camp?* Wait a minute…. Omygod. Omygod. You're not *him?!* Omygod. Are you?!

TOBY Him?

ZOE She told me about the boy from that camp and they were madly in love, and he wrote her a poem. And they made this crazy vow in blood to meet in thirty years—

TOBY Thirty-one.

ZOE It is you! Well, holy shit! Somewhere the gods are laughing. She thought about trying to find you a couple of times, you know—

TOBY Really?

ZOE But I think she felt a bit silly after all these years. I mean what were you, twelve?

TOBY Thirteen.

ZOE But it didn't seem silly to me. It seemed, I don't know, sort of cool. Anyway, she knew the date was coming up.

TOBY It's here.

ZOE It's today? No shit. Well, she said, "with my luck, he'll remember, and turn up, and be this wonderful, handsome hunka man"…

Pause.

What happened, by the way?

TOBY Well, I – I—

ZOE It's a joke! You look great! You look like a friggin' godsend!

TOBY Godsend?

ZOE You've got no idea, you've got no idea what this will mean to her. Shit. I think I'm going to cry. It's so ironic. But that's what she said. He'll show up and that – and that will be the day I pull the big *adios.*

TOBY The big *adios*?

ZOE Oh, shit. I'm being stupid. Zoe, get with it! I saw the flowers. I just assumed…. This is so weird. So, you're just here because of the blood vow thing? You don't know – the situation?

TOBY She's… getting married tomorrow?

ZOE Married?! Where'd you get an idea like that?

TOBY Well, I saw the flowers—

He remembers he's still holding them.

—the flower – and I—

ZOE No, no – she's sick. The kind of sick where you don't get better.

He says nothing.

Anyway, I've been staying with her, keeping her company, contemplating cleaning the oven, but, you know, you run out of things to say after while. And she's not a happy camper these days. But this will give her such a kick. Come on. The place is a bit of a pit, by the way. I suck big time as a housekeeper. Pretend not to notice. Should I tell her you're here, or do you want to surprise her?

She takes his arm, but he doesn't move.

TOBY Don't – don't tell her anything.

He tries to give her the flowers.

You give her these and I'll just—

ZOE You're not going to leave?!

TOBY I don't want to disturb her.

ZOE Disturb her?! The woman is dying. This will be like a gift. For a few minutes she can be thirteen again.

TOBY It's just – it's not that simple. I'm not – I'm not – good at this sort of thing.

ZOE What? Death? Who is?

TOBY Or life.

ZOE What are you good at?

TOBY *(shrugs)* Fiction. Make-believe. Useless trivia. Hopeless romantic fantasies for 200. I won't do well. In there.

ZOE Maybe it's not about you. Maybe it's about her.

TOBY You don't understand. It's complicated, the whole vow and everything. It's not as straightforward as—

ZOE What's wrong with you?!

TOBY *(as if he's about to rhyme off a list)* Well—

ZOE She's not going to sue you for breach of promise for something you said when you were thirteen! She's *sick!* She'd be thrilled to see you. Well, maybe not thrilled, but tickled. Come on. Spend an hour. Spend twenty minutes. Be a mensch.

TOBY I can't.

ZOE Or won't. You're a bit of a gutless wonder, aren't you?

TOBY Oh, yeah.

ZOE Fine. Thanks for nothing. Have a nice life – which is more than some people have to look forward to.

She goes to the door, picks up the single rose, steps inside, leaves the door open so he can hear.

(calls) Mum – I forgot a couple of things. I'll be right back! And guess who showed up—

TOBY Don't!

ZOE That guy who wrote you that poem thirty years ago! But he's too much of a gormless dink to come in and say hello! But you're not missing much! He's not nearly as good looking as you remember!

She leaves the flower and the groceries, comes back out to TOBY where she can't be heard in the house.

Please. It won't kill you. It'll do wonders for your karma. You can talk about good old Camp Wiji-Waji-Whatever-It-Was and the weenie roasts and making out behind the boathouse—

TOBY Oh, we never—

ZOE *(smiles)* Not what I heard… pilgrim.

TOBY stands there, holding the flowers, frozen, at a loss.

TOBY We never did anything.

MARISA *(off, from inside the house)* Brett?… Are you out there?… Brett?

Her voice seems to go right through him. ZOE stands there, looking at him pointedly, then exits.

(off) Brett?

TOBY hesitates, as if he's going to turn and flee… but then he gathers himself, goes to the open door. He looks in. There's no one in the living room.

TOBY Hello?… Marisa?

MARISA *(off)* Brett?… Come here where I can see you.

He goes to the archway.

(off) Brett?… Good Lord, what happened to you?

TOBY Well – uh—

MARISA *(off)* Is it really you?

TOBY *(pause)* It's… it's really me.

Blackout.

End of Act One.

Act Two

Scene One

MARISA enters. Her hair is in a kerchief, but her voice is strong and she walks unassisted. She's clearly not at death's door just yet.

TOBY walks awkwardly beside her, not sure whether to take her arm – or what.

MARISA I can walk, Brett. I'm just dying, I'm not a cripple.

She notices the rose, opens the card.

(reads) "The gang hopes to brighten your day,
By sending this big bouquet."

She looks at the single rose, bemused.

Boy, they must have chipped in at least ten cents each for this.

TOBY stands there holding the big bouquet uncomfortably, holds it out to her.

(perfunctorily) Thanks. You shouldn't have.

She puts it down, goes to an armchair and sits.

God! Why's there a garbage bag in the living room?! Sorry. We had a drunken bacchanal last night. Haven't finished cleaning up.

TOBY A drunken—?

MARISA No, no, I'm mixed up. Wednesday is drunken bacchanal night. Last night was salsa dancing.

TOBY Anyway, garbage doesn't bother me. You should see my room.

MARISA Your room? You live in a room?

TOBY My room in my house. One of many rooms… in my house.

He moves the garbage bag to one side, avoiding her slightly quizzical look.

MARISA This is my daughter's idea of housekeeping. The girl is hopeless.

TOBY She seemed very nice.

MARISA Hopeless.

TOBY I think she's planning to clean the oven.

MARISA *(laughs incredulously)* Alert the media.

TOBY Oh, are you a movie buff?

MARISA Not really. Why?

TOBY It's just – that's a line from a movie. "Arthur." So I thought maybe you were… a buff.

MARISA No. The only movie I've seen in the last couple of years was "Sideways." I liked that.

TOBY You did? I mean, yeah, it was good…

Silence.

I'm sure she'll be back, very soon. Your daughter.

MARISA And then you can go.

TOBY No, no. That's not what I meant. I…

He just stands there, visibly uncomfortable.

MARISA Well then. Sit down. Take a load off. Stay for the evening. Stay for the weekend. How do you like your eggs in the morning?

He doesn't move.

God, Brett. You should see the look on your face. I'm joking. You don't have to stay long. Just a little while.

TOBY Oh, I'll stay as long as – as long as I can.

MARISA *(looks at him intently, which only makes him more uncomfortable)* You look different.

He has no response.

It's all right. You can say it. So do I.

Silence.

Oh, sit. Please. You're making me nervous.

He pulls up a chair, sits self-consciously.

Well, Brett Bradley. I would've bet a million bucks you wouldn't show up today.

TOBY Me too. I knew he wouldn't show up, I mean, I was pretty sure… I wouldn't. It was a long shot.

MARISA But you did.

TOBY I did.

MARISA I'm glad.

TOBY I'm glad too, that you're glad.

MARISA You're not a doctor, are you?

TOBY No?…

MARISA Good. Because your chairside manner is seriously lacking.

TOBY Sorry, I—

MARISA Oh, come on. Move a little closer. I'm not contagious.

He moves the chair closer. Again, she looks at him closely.

Brett, Brett, Brett. I thought you'd forget me after a week. I guess you're a man who takes his blood oaths seriously.

TOBY I guess…

MARISA Look. *(shows him her hand)* I still have a tiny little scar where I stabbed myself with that barrette, do you?

TOBY *(doesn't even look)* No.

MARISA Let's see.

She takes his hand and looks.

Nothing. I left you unscarred. Physically and, I presume, emotionally…

She holds his hand for a moment.

God, Brett, you're all clammy. You're sweating.

TOBY *(pulls his hand away)* Sorry, I…

MARISA No, I'm sorry. I'm just making you uncomfortable. I'm sorry I'm such a bust. This can't be much fun for you.

TOBY No, no. It's fine. It's fun…. It's fine fun.

They both manage a slight laugh.

MARISA Do you want a towel? The linen closet is just down the hall.

He shakes his head, starts to wipe his hand on his shirt – thinks better of it.

Sorry, I can't offer you much – to drink I mean. If you look in the fridge, you might find a cold beer. Or an old beer.

TOBY No, no – I'm fine. Can I get you anything?

MARISA Like what? A martini? A champagne cocktail? A cure?

TOBY I meant a blanket or—?

MARISA Oh, God. I hate this. No—

TOBY Sorry.

MARISA Look, why don't we acknowledge the elephant in the room and get the obvious questions out of the way. Go ahead. Ask away…

He hesitates, doesn't know what to ask.

Okay. Not so fast. I'll answer them one at a time. One. No, I don't know how long I've got. I think they only tell you that in movies. Two. No, I haven't discovered religion. Yet. Three. No, I'm not in pain. I have a regular little Shoppers Drug Mart back there – uppers, downers, sideways-ers – which keeps me trucking along. Life is a pharmacy, old chum. Four. As for my funeral, feel free to say something hilarious and heartbreaking and then scatter my ashes from the Leaning Tower of Pisa while singing "That's Amore." You know – *(starts singing)* "When the moon hits your eye—"

TOBY "Like a big piece a pie—"

MARISA —yadda, yadda. And finally, five – yes, there is something you can do for me. You can stop looking so gloomy – and damp – and earn my everlasting gratitude by talking to me as if I'm a person and not an invalid. Mind you, in my case everlasting may mean only 'til Friday at lunchtime…

He doesn't laugh.

God, Brett. Don't look so horrified. It's called gallows humour. Now quit peppering me with all these questions and tell me about yourself.

TOBY About myself?

MARISA Your hopes, your dreams, your fears…

He looks blank.

Your hobbies?

TOBY *(groping)* Well, there isn't much to tell, really. I, uh, I play a little golf—

MARISA Really? You don't look much like a golfer. What's your handicap?

TOBY Oh, general lack of coordination, I guess.

She laughs more than this warrants.

MARISA You've kept your sense of humour. That's great. Actually, I don't remember you having a sense of humour.

TOBY Thirteen-year-olds don't have senses of humour. They have hormones.

MARISA *(laughs again, almost girlishly)* Oh, we had those, all right. The summer of the Raging Hormones. Sexual tension hung in the air like perfumed smog. Seeping into every exposed inch of skin 'til you tingled all over.... You remember that feeling?

TOBY *(visibly uncomfortable)* Oh. Yeah.... Um, the linen closet?...

MARISA Just down there.

He practically bolts into the hallway.

It seems like only... thirty-one years ago...

She gets up, goes and gets something from a desk drawer. As she looks at it, we realize that it's the other half of the torn photo.

Anyway, thanks for coming. Really. I felt a bit ridiculous even remembering this after all this time.

She pockets the half photo, returns to her chair as he comes back in, rubbing his hands and face with a towel.

I wouldn't want you to think my life has just been a void for thirty-one years, waiting for you to show up. That would be sort of sad.

TOBY I know what you mean.

MARISA You do? So, the fact that you remembered too – well, I guess maybe it's not quite so ridiculous after all.

TOBY Or we're equally ridiculous?

MARISA *(shrugs)* It's strange, what we remember—

TOBY The heart has its reasons—

MARISA Pascal.

TOBY Mmm?

MARISA Pascal. "The heart has its reasons of which reason knows nothing."

TOBY Really? It's not Aristotle? Or Oprah?

MARISA *(laughs)* No, old Pascal. He also said life sucks, and then we die alone.

He just looks at her.

Sorry. There I go, being a wet blanket again. Just when we were starting to loosen up and have fun talking about French philosophers. So who's your favourite?

TOBY French philosopher? Well, Lord Baden Powell, I guess – I Scout, therefore I am.

She looks blank.

Sorry, that was a feeble attempt to blend philosophy humour with cub-scout humour.

MARISA That never works.

TOBY Doomed from the get-go.

MARISA You've changed, haven't you?

TOBY Well, I—

MARISA You're less handsome, but more verbal. You were a thirteen-year-old of few words, mostly of one syllable. That's what made that poem you wrote me so incredible. That you could actually write it. With your own two hands.

TOBY I only used one hand actually, which makes it even more incredible.

She laughs, takes his hand, again making him uncomfortable.

MARISA I loved your hands. They were so tanned and strong and perfect.... Do you remember it? Your poem?

TOBY No, not really. It would probably seem pretty juvenile. Now.

MARISA Maybe. I did like it, though. I loved it – at the time.

TOBY *(withdrawing his hand, reaching for the towel)* Anyway, sorry about the loss of handsomidity. I just woke up one morning and there it was, lying on the pillow. Gone.

MARISA Don't be sorry. I don't mind this version. Of you. I may even prefer this version.

TOBY Really?

MARISA It's like developing a taste for Pinot Noir. As I get older, I find myself strangely drawn to men who are more multisyllabic, and at least willing to attempt French philosopher jokes.

He gets up, perspiring, wiping himself with the towel, pacing.

TOBY Look, um, Marisa – I don't know how to say this. Exactly. I really should – we really should get those flowers in water. Can we back up? To where I came in? There's something I should—

MARISA Stop.

TOBY Stop?

MARISA It's all right. It's my fault. I shouldn't be flirting with you—

TOBY Are you?

MARISA You didn't notice? I must be slipping – oh wait. I am slipping. Into eternity. I almost forgot. For a minute, I almost forgot. Thank you. For that…

Pause.

Anyway, it's a bit tacky on my part. And it's hardly fair, expecting you to flirt with the terminally ill. It's basically a charity flirt for you – there's not much future in it. So, go ahead. I expect you were about to tell me that you're happily married, and—

TOBY Happily married? Oh no, no. I'm not married. I mean, not at the moment, no—

MARISA But you were?

TOBY No, no, actually. No.

MARISA You don't seem quite sure.

TOBY Oh, I'm sure. I'm damn sure. I'd know something like that.

MARISA You're not gay, are you?

TOBY Gayyy? Of course not! Gay! I've had piles of girlfriends. Oodles. Scads. Gazillions. Why would you ask me a question like that?

MARISA I'm dying. I can ask anything. It's like the big carte blanche to quit pussyfooting around. Cut to the nitty-gritty. What are your sexual preferences? How much money do you make? Do you cheat on your income tax? Do you cheat on your wife? Boxers or briefs? What are people going to do if I offend them? Take me off their Christmas card list?

Silence.

I googled you, you know.

TOBY You did?

MARISA You live in Florida now?

TOBY I do. I do – yes. I do. It's… balmy.

MARISA So you came all the way up here and this is what you find? A dying woman trying to flirt and quoting Pascal. What a bummer. Now I really feel guilty. On top of being terminally ill. I hate it when that happens.

TOBY Oh – I had to be here anyway – for a business convention sort of – thing.

MARISA What business?

TOBY Oh, the restaurant business—

She waits.

I own a couple of Red Lobsters.

She looks at him, starts to laugh.

What's so funny? I'm very successful.

MARISA I don't know. It just struck me as funny.

Giggling.

I mean, here I am feeling guilty that you've come all this way on some sort of heartfelt romantic quest, and really I'm just a diversion. An excuse to get you away from the Lobster crowd.

Trying to be jocular, but he isn't laughing.

Hey, lighten up. I'm not insulted. Isn't that half the point of those conventions? To grab a bit on the side? Between Lobster Lectures?

TOBY There's no convention. I just made that up. And this was more than a diversion.... A lot more.

MARISA Aw, gee, Brett. I'm sorry. You should have come sooner.... You should have come a lot sooner. But I'm glad you're here.

TOBY I'm glad too.

Silence.

MARISA I think we covered that already.

Silence.

Hey, come on. This is getting positively maudlin. You're supposed to be cheering me up, and you're doing a piss poor job of it. So, what do you remember from those wild and crazy camp days?

TOBY Not much. I hated it. I was miserable there—

She looks at him.

Except I mean when we were together – doing stuff – the stuff we did together.

MARISA That sounds like the beginnings of a country song – The stuff we did together thirty-one years ago—

TOBY —in the rain—

MARISA *(slipping into some vaguely country melody)* —with our old dog—

TOBY —in our old pickup truck—

MARISA —by the railroad tracks—

TOBY —with the lonesome whistle blowin'—

MARISA —when our hearts were young—

TOBY —and not gay—

MARISA I'll say. And not sick...

Pause.

Sorry. That kind of killed the lyrical momentum.

Silence.

TOBY *(trying to be cheerful)* Hey, this'll cheer you up. Remember that time at camp – a bunch of us were playing on the rope swing, you were there, and that fat kid – I don't remember his name – we dared him to jump, and he came waddling down the hill, and he swung out and the rope came loose—

Laughing.

—and he fell and he bounced, and he kept bouncing and rolling head over heels all the way down the cliff like a human beachball. It was hilarious. The way he… bounced.

MARISA *(not laughing)* I wasn't there for that.

TOBY Yes you were.

She shakes her head.

Really? I thought you were. It was pretty funny.

MARISA It sounds awful. Why would you think I'd find that funny?

TOBY I don't know. I guess it wasn't all that funny – for him.

MARISA What became of him?

TOBY Who knows.

Silence.

Are you sure there's nothing I can get you?

MARISA I'm sure.

Another awkward silence. He glances at his watch.

TOBY Your daughter should be back soon. Does she live here?

MARISA She lives in Italy.

TOBY Italy. Really. I love Italy.

MARISA So, you're an Italy aficionado?

TOBY *Si, si.* I'm an expert on Italian films. Fellini, Anto—

He catches himself.

And, of course, I've been there. Lots of times. *Multo*… times.

MARISA I went right after university. Actually, that's where Zoe was conceived. A little whoops by Lake Como. Anyway, now she's a grad student in Florence, working on an MA, supposedly. But I think she spends all her time with some guy named Paulo. She says he's a chef, but busboy is probably more like it.

TOBY Not necessarily. He could be Mafia.

MARISA Thanks for that.

TOBY Or a gigolo.

MARISA And that. I threw a coin in the Trevi Fountain, which means—

TOBY You'll return some day.

MARISA Mmhm. And I always wanted to go back, but it never happened. So now I'm afraid history will repeat itself with Zoe. She'll have a bambino with Paulo and I won't be there to see it. Or to help. Anyway, she's here with me until… whenever. It's not really fair to her, but, well, I have no one else.

Silence. He's still holding the towel awkwardly, wiping his hands, not sure what to do with it.

TOBY Sorry, I got your towel sort of – wet. Well – I guess, maybe I should – I mean I don't want to tire you out.

MARISA You're not tiring me out. But you can go. You've done your good dead for the day – good *deed* for the day. Boy, Freud could drive a truck through that one.

TOBY Can I help you? Take you to the bedroom? Or—

MARISA On a first date? Cool it, pal.

He has no comeback.

There I go again. Being inappropriate.

TOBY *(remembers, takes out the torn photo)* I brought this. I kept it taped inside my locker all through high school.

She says nothing, takes out the other half, holds them so they fit together.

MARISA Together again after thirty-one years. You take it.

TOBY No, no. I'd rather that you have it. It's you and… yours.

She just looks at it, obviously affected by it.

MARISA I wish we'd made it a twenty-one-year vow, then we'd have had, some time…

TOBY I wish things too… I wish things too. I should go.

Not sure what to do, he leans over, kisses her on the cheek.

She puts her arms around his neck and holds him. As he eases back up, she gets up as well.

No, no, don't get up—

MARISA Is it too much to ask for a hug?

He stands there, frozen.

Hold me like you used to. Please…

He hugs her gingerly.

I won't break.

She hugs him tightly, whispers—

You are my sun,
You are my moon…

She stops – kisses him. The kiss lingers for a moment, as if it may develop into something more.

Then he abruptly breaks it off, steps away—

TOBY I can't…. It's not…

MARISA I'm sorry. I'm sorry. I'm making a complete fool of myself. I'm repulsing you.

TOBY No, no. That's not it. I'm repulsing myself.

MARISA Just go. Please. This is only making things worse. All this sentimental, nostalgic mush.

She picks up the two pieces of photo – crumples them, tosses them aside.

TOBY That's not me.

MARISA It's not me, either. We're not thirteen anymore! We can't go back there…. All I care about is what little time I have left!

TOBY I understand—

MARISA No! You can't possibly understand! It's like – it's like that fat kid bouncing down the cliff – which you found so funny.

TOBY It wasn't funny. It hurt—

MARISA There's no stopping. No turning back. Just bouncing, bouncing, terrified, down into the abyss with no lifeline, no upside surprises. No surprises at all…

TOBY *(going towards the door)* I'm sorry. For everything. And I – I hope that—

MARISA That what? That the drugs will work and I'll die peacefully?!

He's at a loss for a response, starts to open the door.

Please don't go. Can't you just close your eyes? Pretend I'm someone else?…

Torn, he stands there.

Please, Brett…

She holds out her hand to him. He hesitates, slowly walks back towards her.

The phone rings.

TOBY Should I—?

MARISA Leave it.

She takes his hand.

MARISA'S VOICE *(on machine)* Hi, this is Marisa. Leave a message.

The machine beeps.

MAN'S VOICE Hey, Marisa! Surprise! You'll never guess who this is!… It's Brett! Brett Bradley! I'm sitting here at the airport with a three-hour layover. And I had this crazy idea that I'd grab a cab and zip down and see you.

MARISA and TOBY stand there during this, both stunned, momentarily frozen.

I'll hang on, maybe you'll pick up…

She drops TOBY's hand as if it's contaminated, backs away in horror.

TOBY Don't be afraid!

Backing away, she trips and falls, cries out in pain—

Oh, God!

MARISA I've twisted my ankle! *(He moves to help her.)* Don't touch me!

BRETT'S VOICE *(on machine)* Well, I guess you're not there. Too bad. Them's the breaks…

TOBY I'm sorry! I'm sorry!

BRETT'S VOICE *(on machine)* I'll give you my cell number. It's 813-697-4707.

TOBY Let me—

MARISA *(pulls herself up)* Stay away!

BRETT'S VOICE *(on machine)* And my home number in Florida. It's 813-697-4822.

She circles, limping towards the phone, giving TOBY a wide berth.

TOBY I can explain—

BRETT'S VOICE *(on machine)* And my office number is 813-697-4222…

TOBY I—

BRETT'S VOICE Extension 734. Sorry we didn't connect. I hope you're well.

MARISA *(grabs the phone)* Brett!…

But he's hung up.

Damn!

TOBY I can explain. Actually, I can't explain. I—

MARISA Shut up! Who the hell are you?!

TOBY Oh. Toby Boone.

MARISA Who?

TOBY Tobias Boone – the film critic? Former film critic?

She just stares at him.

We were at camp together thirty-one years ago but we never spoke much or at all really in the commonly accepted sense of actually exchanging words which formed sentences – but I've never stopped loving you.... Oh God, why did I say that?!

MARISA What's wrong with you?!

TOBY I don't know. Something I guess, because people keep asking me that.

She hobbles to a chair, keeping her distance.

Can't I get you some ice? Can't I do something?

MARISA Yes! You can tell me what you're doing in my house! What are you? Some sort of demented stalker?!

TOBY No, no. I'm a critic! An unemployed critic, for heaven's sake! Not that that would preclude being a demented stalker, I guess, but—

MARISA So what is this? Some weird, sick game?

TOBY No.

MARISA Some cheap thrill?

TOBY Do I look thrilled?

MARISA No, but you look cheap! Have you no sense of common decency?! Pretending to be someone else! Touching me, *kissing* me – God! If I wasn't already sick I'd be sick!

TOBY I know. It's disgusting.

MARISA What do you mean?! It's disgusting for *me!* It was probably the height of titillation for a pervert imposter creep like you! Has it occurred to you that you have some sort of personality disorder?

TOBY It's crossed my mind.

MARISA So what's the diagnosis? Pathetic Weirdo Nutcase who preys on sick women?

TOBY Go ahead. Call me every name in the book. I don't mind. I'll do anything to make you feel better.

MARISA Feel better?! I'm sitting here with garbage in my living room, a broken ankle thanks to you and one other thing – oh yes, cancer! What can you possibly do to make me feel better?!

TOBY Put out the garbage?

MARISA Is that supposed to be funny?!

TOBY Yes! No! I don't know! I just say things! They just pop out!

MARISA God, my ankle hurts!

TOBY I'm sorry.

MARISA Stop saying you're sorry!

TOBY I don't know what else to say! I don't know what else to do!

MARISA Well, here's an idea – why don't you crawl back under your rock and die.

The phone rings again, startling them both.

MARISA'S VOICE Hi, this is Marisa. Leave a message.

BRETT'S VOICE Hey, it's Brett again. I forgot to give you my email—

MARISA lunges, grabs the phone.

MARISA Brett! Hi!… Yes, it's me. What a nice surprise!… No, I was here. I was just dealing with a… situation…. Thirty-one years, I know…. Actually, I did remember. In fact, it's amazing all the remembering that's going on around here.

Looks at TOBY. He just stands there.

Yes, it's just great to hear from you. Great, great, great…. Me? Oh, I'm… great. Just great. The picture of greatness…. Yes. One daughter…. No, no. Divorced. Eons ago… eons. Ages. Long time ago…

TOBY *(mutters half under his breath)* Idiot.

MARISA You too? Really. That's too bad. Well, divorce is a fact of life, I guess. Like taxes and… whatever…. Death. Yes, thank you. That's the word I was searching for…. The boathouse? Of course I remember. You naughty boy. And I still have that poem you wrote me. You remember it?… Oh, you must—

TOBY He won't remember it—

MARISA *(covers the phone, hisses at TOBY)* Do you mind?!

Back on phone.

So Brett, do you know someone named Toby Boone?… Tubby Bum? Well, he's not exactly tubby, but kind of sly and nondescript…. The kid who fell off the rope swing, and bounced down the cliff – that was him? Do you happen to know if he suffered any permanent psychological damage from that?… Oh, no reason…. Nine out of ten on the loser scale?

Laughs.

I think we're getting warm. Hang on—

TOBY walks to the archway. She covers the phone.

Where are you going?!

TOBY I'm sorry if I frightened you. I'm sorry if I upset you. I'm sorry you're sick. I'm sorry for every bad thing that's ever happened to you – or anybody you know – or anybody else in the *whole stinking, putrid, pointless history of human existence!*

He disappears out through the archway.

MARISA Excuse me! The way out is here!

Back on phone.

No, no, everything's fine. I just have someone here doing… something…

During the following, we hear some rattling around, the sound of cupboards being opened and closed off stage.

Seeing anyone? Me?! Hardly. I mean, no one special at the moment…. I'm not really in relationship mode right now, so I see – different people, so to speak.

She covers the phone and hisses at the archway.

What are you doing out there?!

Back on phone.

Listen, Brett, can I call you back? Soon? I have your numbers. All of them…

Distracted by TOBY's offstage rattlings.

Yes, it's great to hear your voice too. It means a lot to me.... What? Here? Now? No, no. Don't do that. You'll just have to turn around and leave. You'll miss your plane.... No! Please don't come!... Please!... Brett?!...

He's obviously hung up.

Shit!

She yells at the archway.

What do you think you're—?!

TOBY comes back in with a pitcher filled with water. He's gulping a beer.

Well, help yourself. Maybe you'd like some nachos to go with that.

He ignores this, unwraps the flowers and puts them in the pitcher—

TOBY So he's coming. I hope it all works out for you.

MARISA Works out?! Hello! I'm dying! Things don't "work out" for dying people!

TOBY They don't always work out for living people, either.

He pours a bit of the sprinkly stuff in with the flowers.

You should add a little bit of this stuff every couple of days.

He goes to the door, still gulping the beer.

MARISA Did you really think you could pull it off?

TOBY Pull it off?

MARISA Your master plan? The Great Imposter thing?

TOBY I didn't *plan* it! I didn't even want to come in. Your daughter shamed me into it. And when you assumed I was Brett, I thought—

MARISA That you'd have some fun at my expense?

TOBY No.

MARISA Did you think you'd just take on his identity? Insinuate your way into my life?

TOBY No.

MARISA Liar. Into my house?

TOBY No.

MARISA Liar. My bed?

TOBY No.

MARISA Liar. My heart?

He doesn't answer.

Just think. If he hadn't phoned so inconveniently we might have lived happily ever after – i.e. for the two or three weeks I have left. Long enough for you to sweet talk me into changing my will, signing over my house—

TOBY Please. Take a good look. Could I sweet talk anybody into anything?

MARISA *(looks)* You have a point.

TOBY I did it for you.

MARISA Bullshit.

TOBY It's true. I thought if you thought I was Brett it would cheer you up. It would mean something to you. I only had to make it last for a few minutes. Then I'd go. And it would leave you with something to…

MARISA To take to the grave with me?

TOBY If I'd told you who I really was, you'd just have been disappointed, or confused or… whatever you are now.

MARISA Oh, I see. So it was your good deed for the day after all. Fool the invalid. Flirt with the poor, dying woman. Give her a little romantic frisson on her death… chair.

TOBY I don't think of you as a poor, dying woman.

MARISA What do you think of me as? *(He just looks at her.)* What do you think of me as?!

TOBY I think – I think of you as the girl on the rope swing, screaming higher, higher – I think that—
You are my sun,
You are my moon,
You are my shining star…

Locked in my heart is where you'll be
'Til I am where you are.

Silence. She stares at him. He turns to go.

Don't forget the little sprinkly stuff – for the flowers.

MARISA Please stop going on about those stupid flowers! I don't even want them! What do you think I see when I look at them?!

TOBY Death.

MARISA *(surprised)* How do you know that?

TOBY It's what I see, too.

MARISA Then why did you bring them?

TOBY *(shrugs)* It's what people do… in the movies.

He heads for the door and stops abruptly.

But the fact is I didn't bring them! I took them from your doorstep! I switched them! So there! You've got me tabbed just right! I'm precisely the sort of bottom-feeding, rock-crawling, flower-stealing loser you think I am!

But she almost looks amused – not the reaction he was expecting.

MARISA So you actually brought me this? A single rose?

TOBY Yeah. A sappy B movie cliché if ever there was one.

MARISA Never underestimate the effect of a sappy cliché on a dying person.

Silence.

You wrote it, didn't you? The poem?

TOBY *(shrugs)* It was thirty-one years ago. What does it matter now?

MARISA I should've known – I did know, deep down.

She goes to the desk.

Brett was cool, he was hot, he was the perfect boyfriend for thirteen, but he had the poetic sensibility of a wombat.

She takes a piece of paper from the drawer where the photo was, hands it to him.

TOBY God, he spelled shining with two n's! You are my "shinning" star! He didn't even copy it out correctly!

MARISA I know. He couldn't have written that poem any more than he could make French philosopher jokes, however lame.

She catches sight of herself in a mirror.

God, I look so awful!

TOBY No, you look beautiful.

MARISA What's wrong with you?

He doesn't answer. It's almost as if this has become a little joke between them.

Do you mean it? Really? I look all right? If you saw me after thirty-one years—

TOBY Which I did.

MARISA —you wouldn't just puke?

TOBY Which I didn't.

MARISA You did duck out for a while. You could easily have puked. I heard you rattling around back there. What were you doing, anyway?

TOBY Oh, checking out your silverware – but it's not my pattern.

MARISA God! He's coming! I can't face it!

TOBY It'll be all right. You were okay with seeing me when you thought I was him.

MARISA I can't believe I thought that! Even for a minute! You're not remotely like him.

TOBY He could have changed in thirty-one years.

MARISA Not into you.

A beat. He looks at her. Was that actually meant as a compliment?

Anyway, I can't go through a scene like this again.

TOBY It may not play out exactly the same. He probably won't have to towel off.

MARISA Oh, I'm sure he'll be perfectly nice – and perfectly dry – but I can't bear the idea of being pitied and clucked over by some guy who doesn't know what "eon" means.

TOBY It is a two syllable word.

MARISA This isn't funny! I mean, you're an admitted flower thief who misled me and lied to me and could be some criminal rapist axe murderer for all I know – but at least you didn't pity me.

TOBY I'd never pity you.

MARISA Promise?

Silence. She looks in the mirror again.

Oh God, I don't want him to see me like this! I don't want *anybody* to see me like this! Stop looking at me! Go away!

He hesitates and turns towards the door.

Where are you going?! Stay! I mean go – but take me with you!

TOBY Take you…?

MARISA Somewhere. Anywhere. Let's go.

He plops down on the sofa, shaking his head, looking slightly stunned.

That's not a good start.

TOBY Anywhere? Like even Italy?

MARISA Italy. That would be perfect – except I have chemo on Monday. How about – Little Italy? Do you have a car?

He stares at her, a bit dazed.

Sorry, was that question too hard?

TOBY It's just – I thought when he phoned – I just want to be clear – you're asking, you're choosing to go somewhere with me, not him?

MARISA Let's not make a big deal out of it.

TOBY It's a big deal to me.

MARISA *(heads out through the archway)* I'll be right back…. Look, I'm sorry if I overreacted. Before. Some of the things I said were pretty nasty.

TOBY It was perfectly understandable. No harm done.... And you have René Descartes blanche.

She gives him a look and goes.

He sits there, slightly dazed, staring into space.

No harm done...

He suddenly jumps to his feet, starts marching back and forth compulsively, taking deep breaths, jerking his head back and forth as if trying to clear it.

I'm fine. I feel fine. Fine is how I feel. Do a good turn every day. I'll dob, dob, dob...

He sees himself in the mirror.

You talkin' to me?!

He picks up the garbage bag, sticks his finger in his throat, trying to make himself gag.

MARISA comes back in with a pen and paper, sees him bending over the garbage bag, gagging.

MARISA Are you all right?

TOBY *(quickly puts down the bag)* Two thumbs up. Just a touch of pestilence.

MARISA Pestilence? That was my pet word when I was a kid.

TOBY I know. I remember everything about you. I remember things that didn't even happen.

MARISA What are you talking about?

TOBY Oh, I've created whole fantasies about you. I had one today outside on the street. Where you live.

MARISA *(starts trying to write a note)* Hmmm, well, I'm glad to be fantasized about. I guess. Depending on the fantasy... and the fantasizer.

TOBY Oh, this wasn't just some tawdry B movie fantasy where I stride in and twirl my moustache and you turn to jelly like that –

He snaps his fingers ineffectually and tries again.

– like that – and I sweep you off your feet and carry you off to my lair and – and – you know—

MARISA Easy, boy.

TOBY No, no, this was an Oscar calibre fantasy, an Oscar Wilde calibre fantasy. This was a fantasy with texture and nuance and character development and plot twists and a memorable cameo appearance by Helena Bonham Carter—

MARISA I have no earthly idea what you're talking about.

TOBY – she of the lovely bum bum. I have a bit of a thing for Helena.

MARISA I'm sure she feels the same way. *(quickly scribbling the note)* Perhaps you can tell me all about it another time.

TOBY *(looks unsteady, flops down on the sofa again)* There won't be another time.

MARISA There might be, if you play your cards right. I still have a few good days left in me. Although I'm not so sure about you.

She finishes the note.

There. Can we go? Now?

But he doesn't budge. He carries on a bit dreamily, almost as if he hasn't heard her.

TOBY You were untouchable, you were unattainable, you were about to march down the aisle with Golden Boy, as soon as he was done with Big Bertha.

MARISA With who?

TOBY But I wooed you with allusions to "Citizen Kane" and quotes from "Casablanca" and – other stuff – and slowly, inexorably, I won you over with bumbling charm and cub jokes until you agreed to run off to Italy with me. And you gazed into my eyes and – and—

MARISA Turned to jelly?

TOBY Like that—

He tries to snap his fingers a couple of times, ineffectually. He looks at them as if they're someone else's fingers.

Why won't they snap?!

He tries again. There's obviously something not quite right about him.

MARISA Are you drunk?

TOBY On one beer? Madam, you jest.

He lurches abruptly to his feet and stumbles.

Do you have any rope?

MARISA Rope? Why?

TOBY *(slurring his words slightly now)* Because if you're going to appreciate my fantasy, featuring you – and Helena in a supporting role – you have to go back to the very seed of the idea. I was tying a clove hitch, see, for personal and private reasons, which we needn't go into—

MARISA You are drunk!

TOBY *(wielding an imaginary rope)* You make a loop like a lake, or a kidney-shaped pool – and a snake pokes its nose up out of the lake, like so – hello, snake! And winds itself sinuously around a tree, and—

MARISA That's not a clove hitch. That's something else, a bowline or—

TOBY Fine. Destroy my fantasy… destroy my fantasy…

He gets up, takes a couple of unsteady steps towards the door.

MARISA What's wrong with you?!

He crashes to the floor.

Omygod! Did you take something back there?!

TOBY *(takes her hand, giggles woozily)* Your perfect little hand.

MARISA Did you find some pills back there?! Did you?!

TOBY I paid a little visit to your Shoppers Drug Mart.

MARISA Oh, God!

TOBY But I didn't have my Optimum-mum card.

MARISA What did you take?!

TOBY My Opti-bum-bum Card.

MARISA *(slaps him across the face)* Tell me!

TOBY Uppers… downers… *(giggles giddily)* Sideways-ers!…

MARISA Idiot!

TOBY That's funny…

MARISA Damn you! Damn you!

TOBY Damn me.

MARISA This is all wrong! I'm the one who's sick! I'm the one who's been told to avoid stress!

He's clutching her hand, but she pries herself free, grabs the phone and punches 9-1-1.

And this is very stressful!

TOBY *(lying there, in more of a stupour now)* Just let me go… don't want to be any trouble.

MARISA *(on phone)* Ambulance! Ambulance!… *(waiting)*

TOBY *(getting progressively more slurred and sleepy)* Just let me get to the edge of the cliff… won't be a Tubby nuisance to you anymore.

MARISA Shut up!

TOBY Sorry.

MARISA *(on phone)* Yes! I need an ambulance! Now!… 207 Elmhurst! Corner of Maple! There's an idiot here who's taken some pills!

TOBY *(sleepily, dreamily)* I'm the idiot…

MARISA I don't know! It could be any number of things!

TOBY Uppers… downers…

MARISA Just send somebody!—

TOBY Sideways-ers…

MARISA Please! Now!…

TOBY Almost there… almost at the edge…

MARISA His relationship to me?! He has no relationship to me! He's, he's—

TOBY Your shinning star.

MARISA Yes, I'll stay on the line. Please, tell them to hurry!

TOBY No hurry…

She sets the phone down, huddles down beside TOBY, who's lying there, semi-comatose now.

MARISA Talk to me!

TOBY Told me… to shut up…

She takes his head, cradles it on her lap.

MARISA I take it back. Talk. Tell me a cub joke.

TOBY *(points woozily)* There's a light there… a bright, shining light—

MARISA No! There's no light. It's dark. Don't go there! Toby!

TOBY *(smiles sleepily)* You said my name. Tobee, or not Tobee. That's funny.

MARISA No, it's not! *(at phone)* Please hurry!

TOBY Bouncing, bouncing – over the precipice…

MARISA No! Don't go!

TOBY Pre-ci-pice… has three syllables…

MARISA Stay with me.

TOBY Pes-ti-lence… has… has…

MARISA Three syllables! Keep talking!

She shakes him.

Talk to me!… Talk to me!… Toby*!*

But he's silent now, unconscious.

(grabs phone, in a panic) He's stopped talking! What should I do?!… I am talking! Please hurry! Toby!? Please don't do this to me!

He doesn't respond.

Is this my fault? Is it because I called you a pathetic weirdo nutcase? Come on!

She puts the phone down, presses on his stomach, kind of bounces on him, trying to make him vomit.

I've said far worse things to people and they didn't go and take pills!

She yells at the phone.

Hurry! Please!—

To TOBY, cradling his head now.

Listen – are you listening?! – and this will sound ridiculous, because I've only known you for forty-five minutes, and for half that time you were pretending to be someone else, so that's really only twenty-two and a half minutes. And in that time you made me feel like a fool, and got me absolutely furious, and you misquoted Pascal *and stole my drugs!* – but you almost made me laugh a couple of times and we made up
a country and western song – and I know that's not much to build on—

During the following, as she talks, a bright, glowing light comes up on one side, and TOBY gets up – as if in slow motion – and starts to move slowly away from her towards the light, as if his soul is leaving his body. Unaware of this, MARISA continues talking to the spot where he was, as if she's still cradling his head.

But we had a thirty-one-day relationship once, of sorts, so why not take another shot? Who knows, we may only have another thirty-one days, but we could do a lot in that time if we got up early. Are you a morning person? *(She shakes "him.")* Please answer me!

Moving slowly away, he pauses, reacts slightly, as if perhaps he has heard her.

We could rent every movie Helena Bonham Carter ever made. Not that I can actually remember any of them right now—

TOBY *(staring at the light)* "Room With a View."

MARISA —and order pizza and stay up all night watching them.

But he resumes moving ever so slowly away towards the light.

And then at dawn we could watch the sun come up and clean my oven. Please laugh. Please do something!

She shakes "him." Again, he pauses, reacts slightly.

Is it true what you said? That you never stopped loving me? Not that I'm asking you to love me, because Lord knows I'm not very lovable these days, but I have a journey to make, and I damn well don't want to make it alone—

Murray Furrow
photo by Dan Pritchard

But TOBY continues moving away, gazing at the light, drawn towards it.

We begin to hear the distant sound of a siren, growing gradually louder during the following.

And Pascal was wrong. We don't have to die alone! We don't! And you made me feel something, which is a whole lot better than feeling just cold, dead nothing, so don't you die on me you stupid, stupid, stupid man!

TOBY *(continues to drift inexorably towards the light, which seems to be getting brighter)* You are my sun.... You are my moon...

Shaking him, getting no response, she loses it, breaks down, grabs the pitcher, flings the flowers at "him."

MARISA Fine! Take your stupid dead flowers with you!

She suddenly has an idea, grabs the sachet of plant food, pours it in his mouth, dumps in water, as if forcing it down his throat.

The siren is getting louder, closer. She almost has to shout over it now.

Swallow it! Swallow it! Now puke! Damn you! *Puke!*

Red, flashing light comes through the window now, playing on the walls, the siren wailing, making the room seem like the gateway to hell.

Puke...

Done in by her furious exertion, she seems to give up, sags to the floor in a state of collapse.

The siren gives a last shriek, stops. Almost eery silence. Everything freezes for a moment.

TOBY stares at the bright light.

He quivers ever so slightly once or twice, as if trying to suppress a cough.

You blew it, you know. Hey, I'm every man's dream – a short-term relationship, no commitment required, and an ironclad escape clause.

A beat. The bright light starts to fade. TOBY backs away from it, slowly, then more quickly – precisely retracing his steps backwards to the exact position he was lying in, sprawled on the floor – as if his spirit is re-entering his body.

Unaware of this, MARISA is huddled, bent over, breathless, crying. She's given up.

Oh, I know you had your Oscar-calibre fantasy – and reality turned out to be a big, fat pile of garbage and pestilence and dying – but it was life, you know. Life, which comes with crap attached. And you should have tried it for once… for once…

TOBY twitches, jerks, emits a profound, moannnnnnn from the very depths of his being.

(jumps, completely startled) Shit!

He starts to shake, choke, gag… she knows what's coming.

Oh, shit –

She grabs the garbage bag, lifts his head and shoves it in the bag – holds him as he retches violently, convulsively, cataclysmically.

Finally done, he flops down on the floor, gasping. MARISA also lies back, drained, exhausted.

TOBY comes awake, looks around woozily.

TOBY Helena?

MARISA Helena! It's Marisa!

TOBY Marisa? Oh… Marisa.

Utterly dazed, he looks at the red flashing lights filling the room.

Is this hell?

MARISA It was.

TOBY Why are we lying on the floor?

MARISA I'll tell you about it some time.

TOBY I had the weirdest dream. You were, well, sort of humping me—

MARISA Dream on.

TOBY And screaming at me and slapping me and trying to push me over a cliff – as if you hated me.

MARISA *(takes his hand)* I don't hate you.

TOBY That's good.

MARISA I'm still… on the fence about you.

TOBY Oh… could that be a fence – in Italy?

MARISA They tend to be stone walls in Italy.

TOBY I know. I've seen them. In the movies.

They lie there, both completely wiped, looking at each other, holding hands.

We hear a car door slam. A beat, then there's a sharp banging on the door.

MAN *(off)* Marisa!?… It's Brett!

TOBY & MARISA *(together)* Oh, shit.

Blackout.

We hear an upbeat version of "That's Amore."

Scene Two

The scrim is back in place – an image of Florence now projected on it.

TOBY sits downstage at a little café table with a bottle of Chianti. He's lost in thought, humming/singing "That's Amore" to himself. There's a suitcase beside him.

ZOE enters behind him, slightly in shadow.

ZOE Hey.

He turns, stares at her. For just a second he's speechless, almost as if he's thinking – MARISA? ZOE sees this too.

It's me. Not a ghost. Sorry. I keep doing that.

She joins him at the table. We see now that she's visibly pregnant.

Murray Furrow and Jan Alexandra Smith
photo by Dan Pritchard

TOBY It's okay. I was just thinking… about her.

ZOE And singing.

TOBY I wasn't singing.

ZOE Yes you were. You're turning into a regular Italian cliché. Lounging in the piazza, drinking wine, singing away. Next you'll be pinching women's bums.

TOBY You know, I always thought that song – the one I wasn't singing – went "when the moon hits your eye like a big piece a pie that's amore." But there isn't really any phase of the moon that looks like a piece of pie, and having given the matter considerable thought, I realize it's probably – "when the moon hits your eye like a big *pizza* pie" – What do you think?

ZOE I think, either way – it's amore.

TOBY Yeah. It is. It was. Well, to amore.

She pours herself a small glass of wine.

Should you—?

ZOE In my delicate condition? One sip won't hurt.

TOBY To Marisa.

ZOE To Mum.

They drink. A beat of silence.

So, you've got her?

TOBY *(pats the suitcase)* In here. In her little box.

ZOE And you're really going to do it? Dump her off the Leaning Tower of Pisa?

TOBY Don't say dump. Say… scatter. It sounds more elegant.

ZOE Crazy is what it sounds. I mean, I've heard of people who want their ashes scattered in the Grand Canyon or someplace sensible – but the Leaning Tower of Pisa!

TOBY It's what she wanted. And I promised her.

ZOE But it's crowded there! They'll probably land on some German tourist's head! *(gesticulating Germanically)* Ach! Some dumkopf is dumping ze zawdust on mein dumkopf!

They're both laughing.

I'm terrible. Zoe! This is no laughing matter!

TOBY She wouldn't mind. She liked to laugh.

ZOE She got to laugh, thanks to you. You know, when she got sick, I went back and I did my best—

TOBY She knew that.

ZOE But I couldn't give her what you could. You came along and kind of took me off the hook. Put a little, I don't know, pizzaz, back in her life for a bit.

TOBY Ninety-three days. And it was mutual.

ZOE And she loved it here. With you. With us.

TOBY I hope so.

ZOE You know she did. And the funny thing is these ninety-three days – riding around on the scooter, shopping for baby things, going to Lake

Como, just hanging out – these were the best times I ever had with her. Ever. So you gave us both a gift. Heck, she even came to like Paulo.

He gives her a look.

Well, tolerate. So, well, thanks. *Grazie mille.*

TOBY *Prego.*

Laughs, hesitates.

Well, I guess this is *arrivederci.*

She looks taken aback.

I've booked a flight from Pisa – back home.

ZOE Back home? But what will you do?

TOBY Oh, the usual social whirl – hobnob with Spielberg, clean the oven, work on my book—

ZOE The Crap Crap Crap book?

TOBY I may change that. Actually, I've been thinking of writing, well, about this.

ZOE A ninety-three-day love story.

TOBY Or thirty-one years and ninety-three days, depending how you look at it.

We hear a scooter's beep beep.

ZOE It's Paulo—

TOBY *(waves) Ciao,* Paulo!

ZOE See, you even wave like an Italian now. I gotta go. We're short staffed at the café.

She stands.

So, when are you coming back to see the *bambino*?

TOBY Well… one of these days. Someday.

ZOE No, that's not good enough.

She hesitates.

She made me promise to do something too.

TOBY Do something?

ZOE It's the last thing she said to me. Whatever you do, don't let him go back to that damn room. He'll just mope around and obsess and fantasize about this for the next thirty-one years. So take care of business in Pisa, and come back here.

He hesitates.

I'm serious. We'll get you a cardigan and slippers and you can be a surrogate grandpa. And, hey, there's that little place in the hills that we're dying to rent. We can't really afford it – but if you shared it. There's a spare room, well, a spare closet. You could sit and look out at the Tuscan countryside and write to your heart's content.

TOBY You're saying it has "A Closet with a View"?

ZOE *(allows him a tolerant laugh)* She wanted you to be happy, you know. To live. To meet someone else. And you know what they say about Italian women—

TOBY They have a thing for broken down ex-film critics in cardigans and slippers?

ZOE Okay. Skip the cardigan and slippers. So, *(taking something out of her bag)* give me your hand.

TOBY *(realizes what she's up to)* What? No! Don't be silly!

ZOE Come on. It's a family tradition.

TOBY This is ridiculous.

But she jabs his finger with a safety pin. He yelps.

ZOE Wuss. *(she pricks herself, takes his hand)* Now promise you'll come back. *(squeezes his hand) Promise.*

TOBY *(pause)* I promise.

ZOE And you know what happens if you break a blood oath.

TOBY Actually, I don't.

ZOE Well, I don't either. But it's really, really bad.

Another beep from the scooter. She hugs him tightly, turns to go.

TOBY I'm bleeding.

ZOE That's the point, silly.

Murray Furrow
photo by Dan Pritchard

She rests her hand on the suitcase for a second, in silent goodbye to her mother, exits. TOBY stands there for a moment, drains his wine, grabs the suitcase, pauses.

TOBY *(to the audience)* Just trying to think of a snappy exit line… oh, well.

He heads off – stops abruptly, turns and stares intently. Something has caught his eye.

You won't believe this, but a woman in a long, flowered dress walked by over there, and for just a second I could have sworn it was Helena Bonham Carter—

He looks again and shrugs.

Ah, who cares.

He heads off in the other direction, lugging the suitcase and singing to himself.

"When you walk in a dream
But you know you're not dreaming, signore
Scuza mi, but you see,
Back in old Napoli – that's amore…
That's amore…"

Blackout.

The End.

Raised in Ottawa, Douglas Bowie fell into a writing career when he entered a CBC TV contest on a whim while working for a local ad agency. His teleplay "Who Was the Lone Ranger?" won a top prize and launched a thirty-year career, during which he has written a wide range of film and TV dramas. These include "The Man Who Wanted To Be Happy," "The Newcomers," "The Boy in Blue" (starring Nicolas Cage), "Obsessed," the mini-series "Chasing Rainbows," the Gemini Award winning "Love and Larceny," "Grand Larceny," and the Christmas perennial "Must Be Santa" (starring Dabney Coleman).

He won an ACTRA Award for the hit CBC mini-series "Empire, Inc.," and a Gemini Award for an outstanding body of work in television. He edited the book *Best Canadian Screenplays*, and added playwriting to his repertoire in the '90s. His plays include the award-winning comedy *The Noble Pursuit*, *!SGODSDOGS!*, *Goodbye, Piccadilly*, *Love and Larceny* (the musical), and *Rope's End*. He lives in Kingston and is currently playwright-in-residence at the Thousand Islands Playhouse.